Identity-Native Infrastructure Access Management

Access Management

Preventing Breaches by Eliminating Secrets and Adopting Zero Trust

Ev Kontsevoy, Sakshyam Shah, and Peter Conrad

Beijing · Boston · Farnham · Sebastopol · Tokyo

Identity-Native Infrastructure Access Management

by Ev Kontsevoy, Sakshyam Shah, and Peter Conrad

Published by O'Reilly Media, Inc., 1005 Gravenstein Highway North, Sebastopol, CA 95472.

O'Reilly books may be purchased for educational, business, or sales promotional use. Online editions are also available for most titles (*http://oreilly.com*). For more information, contact our corporate/institutional sales department: 800-998-9938 or *corporate@oreilly.com*.

Acquisitions Editor: Jennifer Pollock   **Indexer:** Ellen Troutman-Zaig
Development Editor: Jeff Bleiel   **Interior Designer:** David Futato
Production Editor: Aleeya Rahman   **Cover Designer:** Karen Montgomery
Copyeditor: nSight, Inc.   **Illustrator:** Kate Dullea
Proofreader: Heather Walley

September 2023:   First Edition

Revision History for the First Edition
2023-09-12:   First Release

See *http://oreilly.com/catalog/errata.csp?isbn=9781098131890* for release details.

978-1-098-13189-0

[LSI]

Table of Contents

Preface

The challenge of securing infrastructure is no secret. As an organization scales and more people need access, a lush forest of policies and tools grows organically, resulting in both inconvenience and vulnerability across the entire infrastructure.

This is very bad.

This book provides theory and real-world advice to help organizations step up to the new challenge of securing infrastructure: no secrets! The following chapters consider all aspects of identity-based access management, addressing topics from identity proofing to auditing. By bringing identity-based, unified policy to both humans and machines, this book aims to solve vulnerability and inconvenience in one stroke.

After all, the point of infrastructure access is to let the right people in so they can work together easily.

Who Should Read This Book

As a company grows, infrastructure access becomes more important and more difficult. Secret-based perimeter defenses don't scale. This book is for anyone facing the challenges of defending an ever-growing infrastructure, whether on-premises, in the cloud, or both. The book is accessible to a reader with a modicum of technical skill and a passing familiarity with IT, networking, and the Linux command line.

Whether you're an executive, an IT policymaker, or a DevOps engineer, if you have responsibility for helping secure heterogeneous computing infrastructure, this book is for you.

Goals of the Book

The world is changing. Infrastructure will continue to evolve. New tools, platforms, and technologies will spring into use alongside legacy products and services. Securing infrastructure will become more and more crucial, but also more difficult. The old approaches don't work anymore. Without a basis in proven identity, vulnerabilities and friction inevitably develop, leading to increasing cost and a breakdown in trust.

This book outlines an approach designed to bring trust back, providing chains of trust and chains of proof that reduce vulnerability and human error while making access policies easier to follow. By rebuilding trust, we aim to make it easier for people to work together securely. In fact, security should be something the average user doesn't have to think about.

Navigating This Book

This book begins with the basics of identity-based security, proceeds through the foundations of connectivity, authorization and authentication, then winds up with a real-world example and a call to action. Here are brief descriptions of the chapters:

Chapter 1, "Introduction: The Pillars of Access"
> The weaknesses of traditional security models and how true identity-native infrastructure access solves these problems by eliminating human error and the attacker's ability to pivot.

Chapter 2, "Identity"
> This chapter defines and discusses identity, the challenge of proving and representing identity, and a method for bringing physical identity into the digital realm.

Chapter 3, "Secure Connectivity"
> This is a discussion of the importance of secure connectivity and the principle of zero trust, showing why it is important for identity-native infrastructure access.

Chapter 4, "Authentication"
> We talk about authentication schemes, with an eye toward using existing and new authentication techniques to support the identity-native principles discussed throughout the book.

Chapter 5, "Authorization"
Here are a variety of authorization frameworks, showing how they can work together to bring consistent policy enforcement across infrastructure, including bringing data protection to the hardware level.

Chapter 6, "Auditing"
This explains why auditing is an important complement to identity-native access policy, including an example of a typical attack and how the principles discussed in the book can help defend infrastructure.

Chapter 7, "Scaling Access: An Example Using Teleport"
Here is a real-world example using Teleport and other open source tools and techniques to implement identity-native infrastructure access policy at scale.

Chapter 8, "A Call to Action"
This final chapter is a look at the state of the world, a glance forward, and a call to action: How can we create the best possible future for trust in technology?

Conventions Used in This Book

The following typographical conventions are used in this book:

Italic
Indicates new terms, URLs, email addresses, filenames, and file extensions.

`Constant width`
Used for program listings, as well as within paragraphs to refer to program elements such as variable or function names, databases, data types, environment variables, statements, and keywords.

O'Reilly Online Learning

 For more than 40 years, *O'Reilly Media* has provided technology and business training, knowledge, and insight to help companies succeed.

Our unique network of experts and innovators share their knowledge and expertise through books, articles, and our online learning platform. O'Reilly's online learning platform gives you on-demand access to live training courses, in-depth learning paths, interactive coding environments, and a vast collection of text and video from O'Reilly and 200+ other publishers. For more information, visit *https://oreilly.com*.

How to Contact Us

Please address comments and questions concerning this book to the publisher:

O'Reilly Media, Inc.
1005 Gravenstein Highway North
Sebastopol, CA 95472
800-889-8969 (in the United States or Canada)
707-829-7019 (international or local)
707-829-0104 (fax)
support@oreilly.com
https://www.oreilly.com/about/contact.html

We have a web page for this book, where we list errata, examples, and any additional information. You can access this page at *https://oreil.ly/identity-native-infrastructure-access*.

For news and information about our books and courses, visit *https://oreilly.com*.

Find us on LinkedIn: *https://linkedin.com/company/oreilly-media*

Follow us on Twitter: *https://twitter.com/oreillymedia*

Watch us on YouTube: *https://youtube.com/oreillymedia*

Acknowledgments

The authors would like to thank the team at O'Reilly Media for helping them through the process of writing this book. Our editor Jeff Bleiel was instrumental in getting this across the finish line. Also, thanks to Jennifer Pollock, Aleeya Rahman, and Carol Keller.

Thank you to Jack Naglieri and Ken Westin for their contributions to Chapter 6. Thank you to Sasha Klizhentas for reviewing the access control material and to Prabath Siriwardena for additional technical review.

## CHAPTER 1

Introduction: The Pillars of Access

Access to computing infrastructure becomes both more important and more difficult at scale. This book explores methods to make access easier, more scalable, and more secure.

Computing infrastructure has a very broad meaning, but what we mean in this book is computing resources located in cloud environments, on-premises, or colocated data centers, and even Internet of Things (IoT) devices on public networks. The definition of computing resources includes hardware such as servers, networking, and storage, as well as infrastructure software such as databases, message queues, Kubernetes clusters, monitoring dashboards, continuous integration/continuous delivery (CI/CD), and other DevOps tooling.

Controlled access to this complex panoply has historically relied on the notion of a network perimeter and user credentials, the digital versions of what people use to control access to their homes: a door and a set of keys. A user credential, such as a password or a private key, is nothing more than a secret piece of information that unlocks a specific perimeter. All these secrets are just data—like any data, they can be lost, shared, copied, stolen, or even sold. Neither a physical key nor a digital key guarantees the identity of someone attempting access. Simply being in possession of the key allows access. When access management relies on secrets, it is giving access not to a client, but to the secret itself. This makes a stolen secret very powerful.

Like most perimeter-based access control implementations, the front door lock on a house does nothing once an intruder gains access. Anyone with the single key to the house has access to all the valuables inside. Additional perimeter defenses inside the home have the same fundamental problem. Once an attacker is inside, everything is accessible.

Corporate networks that rely on secrets and perimeter defenses have the same weakness but worse. Perimeter-based security based on secrets is inadequate because:

- The keys can be stolen, lost, or shared with someone legitimate and duplicated secretly. In other words, secrets are vulnerable to human error.

- As infrastructure complexity increases, there can be too many entry points to protect, increasing operational overhead and leading to a growing thicket of vulnerabilities.

- There can be many users with different access requirements for different resources, making it difficult to grant only the right access to every user.

- An intruder who manages to gain access can easily pivot the attack to adjacent resources inside the perimeter, wreaking damage along the way.

As a company grows, a secure access model based on a perimeter and secrets does not scale. All of the weaknesses above illustrate the same pattern: an attacker exploits human error, then pivots to get everywhere.

Your computing infrastructure may consist of cloud accounts with API endpoints, virtual machines (VMs), databases, Kubernetes clusters, monitoring dashboards, and CI/CD tools. You may even have traditional data centers with the same resources running in them, and every single resource requires its own access. Configuring connectivity, authentication, authorization, and audit for every resource usually involves maintaining a myriad of configuration files, each with its own compliance requirements and syntax. As the number of resources grows, the complexity of managing access to these components becomes unsustainable—and the cost of a configuration error becomes enormous.

In this chapter, we begin the discussion of identity-native infrastructure access by showing how every breach or attack relies on the very characteristics that traditional security models encourage, reviewing the pillars of infrastructure access. We will lay out the ways that true identity-native infrastructure access solves all these challenges by eliminating the foundation that most infrastructure attacks rely upon: human error and the attacker's ability to pivot.

Most Attacks Are the Same

Most infrastructure attacks follow the same *human error + pivot* pattern:

1. The attacker first gains a foothold into company-owned computing resources by exploiting *human error*.

2. The attacker then *pivots* to gain access to adjacent computing systems on the same network.

While human errors can be minimized with security training, rigorous recruiting, and other processes, they cannot be eliminated entirely. Humans will reliably be humans. Humans design vulnerable web applications, click malicious email attachments, leave their laptops on the subway, and commit API keys into public Git repositories. These errors and others leave a trail of exploitable vulnerabilities.

Notice how every security-related human error revolves around some kind of secret. Passwords, private encryption keys, API keys, browser cookies, and session tokens are all hubs for human error. Every secret is a potential entry point for a malicious actor. Whenever a new secret is introduced into a computing environment, the probability of a breach increases. This probability may seem insignificant at first, and a successful breach may be unlikely in a small company; but as organizations scale, it becomes a question of *when* and not *if.*

While a secret such as a password is intended to prove the identity expressed by the username, it does no such thing. Secrets-based access assumes that only the authorized person can possess the secret, but we know this is not true. A secret confers all the benefits of identity on an entity without any way to perform true authentication or authorization. Anybody with possession of a secret can pretend to be someone else. In that sense, the common term *identity theft* is misleading because what actually happens is a *secret theft*. A true identity cannot be shared, copied, or stolen.

The probability of any single human making an error that leads to a compromised secret is relatively small, especially with a competent engineering team and a strong security culture. The introduction of robust processes and secret management solutions also reduce the probability of a secret leakage to an extremely low number, but they never bring it down to zero. In practice, the difference between a low number and zero is enormous when an organization operates at scale.

To use memory corruption in a server as an analogy, the probability of a bit flip is extremely low. But as your infrastructure footprint expands and data volumes continue to grow, eventually there will be bit flips happening every minute. That's why error correction code is mandatory at scale: it converts the probability of a bit flip from a very small number to zero. This happens for all kinds of low-probability events at scale. In a large data center, full-time employees are hired to replace hard drives all day, despite each drive having an expected lifespan of three years or more.

Reliance on a secret for access is similar. The probability of a human leaking a secret by mistake may seem small. As infrastructure and teams grow, that small probability inevitably increases. As infrastructure becomes larger and more complex, the surface area of secrets becomes enormous, and the aggregated probability of a compromised secret becomes inevitable. That is why in a modern cloud native infrastructure the mere presence of a secret is considered a vulnerability.

It may be tempting to reduce the risk of a leaked secret by introducing more rigid processes. Draconian security procedures, while they provide a comforting illusion of safety, make engineers less productive and create incentives for bad behavior. Hard-to-use security measures lead people to use shorter passwords, build their own backdoors into infrastructure, keep secure sessions open for longer than needed, try to minimize the security team's involvement in decision making, and take other shortcuts. Even the people who make the most earnest attempts to follow a difficult procedure will end up making a mistake eventually.

It's not the people who are the problem. It's the secrets themselves. Secrets are just data; data is vulnerable to theft, loss, and copying.

Companies such as Google and other so-called hyperscalers were among the first to face this reality, and have come up with a more scalable access architecture that hinges on two crucial patterns:

- No secrets
- Zero Trust

This book covers these two patterns, explaining how they scale in real time with infrastructure without increasing the attack surface area or the probability of a breach.

No secrets means no passwords, keys, or tokens. Eliminating secrets helps scale secure access because without secrets, there's nothing to compromise, so human error is no longer exploitable. Instead of relying on secrets, access is based on identity itself.

Zero Trust means that every user, device, application, and network address is inherently untrusted. There's no perimeter because there's no "inside" where entities are trusted. In a Zero Trust access model, every network connection is encrypted, every session must be authenticated, every client must be authorized, and the audit log is kept for every client action. *With Zero Trust, every computing resource can safely run using a public IP address on an untrusted public network.*

Zero Trust greatly reduces the chance of pivot once an attacker gains control over a single machine and reduces the "blast radius" of an attack to just the one system initially compromised.

Together, no secrets and Zero Trust help neutralize the human error + pivot pattern. With no secrets, human error doesn't introduce vulnerabilities. With Zero Trust, there's no "inside" to get to, so pivoting becomes meaningless. This gives us the freedom to think about access itself.

Access

Access enables people, software, and hardware to work together securely. At its heart, access is a collection of privileges or permissions that allow a *subject* (a client) to perform certain actions on an *object* (a computing resource) for a period of time. Access control means mediating requests by subjects, often users, to access objects, using *rights* that determine the kind of access a specific subject is granted to a specific object. The intention is to control every access event within a system, protecting data and resources from unauthorized disclosure or modifications while ensuring access by legitimate users.

Infrastructure access management is the ability to define and enforce how any client works with any resource. Managing access is the foundation of security in computer infrastructure, governing the use of all hardware and software, and how information is transferred, processed, and stored.

Generally, managed access is *remote* because it involves communication among different machines. In modern infrastructure at scale, it's rare for someone to work only on a single, isolated machine. Remote access management is based on four pillars:

Secure connectivity
Secure communication over an untrusted network

Authentication
Proof of a client's identity

Authorization
Specifying the actions a client can perform

Audit
A record of real-time and historical events

These four components ensure that the right client has the right kind of access to protected resources, and that it's possible for the right others to see what's going on. The next sections provide a quick look at why each pillar is important. Subsequent chapters go into more detail about each one.

Secure Connectivity

Secure connectivity is the first pillar of access. A secure connection must be established before authentication can take place. To access a protected resource securely, an entity must be able to exchange messages without fear of interception.

The legacy approach to connectivity relied on perimeter security, when encryption was needed only for messages leaving the network perimeter, also known as the local area network (LAN) or virtual private cloud (VPC). Anyone within the LAN or VPC was trusted. As infrastructure grows, the network becomes more complicated. Using virtual private networks (VPNs) and firewalls to stitch together perimeters to protect trusted areas becomes extremely challenging and leaves more and more holes.

Even in the best case, perimeter-based security doesn't work because it makes you vulnerable to attacker pivots. Interestingly, security is not the only argument against the perimeter. As more and more external services need connections into private networks, firewalls are basically just speed bumps. Effectively, the perimeter died a long time ago.

That means there can be no such thing as a trusted network. This is what *Zero Trust* means. Encryption, authentication, authorization, and audit can't rely on the network anymore and must shift from the network to the application layer. Requests can no longer be processed based on whether they're on a trusted network. The network itself becomes untrusted, meaning that communication must be end-to-end encrypted at the session level.

Thankfully, the technologies for this were invented a long time ago and are used for secure communications across the internet. All of us are already using them for online banking or shopping. We simply need to properly apply the same Zero Trust principles to our computing environments *inside* the LAN or VPC, not just on a perimeter.

Authentication

Authentication means proving identity. A person, computer, service, or other client requesting access to a protected resource must be able to prove it is who it says it is. When you see a login screen, that's one type of authentication. Authentication must be kept separate from authorization, so that an entity's permissions can be updated if its role changes. Authentication does not determine what an entity is allowed to do. Authentication only asserts identity.

Verifying passwords is a popular authentication method, but it's inadequate for proving identity. After all, password-based authentication merely indicates possession of the secret itself and does not prove the bearer's identity. Authentication must get to the heart of identity, which is a more difficult task. How do you prove the true identity of a person in the digital realm?

One attempt at proving identity is *multifactor authentication* (MFA), which generally uses two or three different kinds of secrets to establish proof. This pattern is sometimes called *know + have + are*, and often means a password (something you know), a one-time token generated by a separate device (something you have), and your biological traits (something you are). Unfortunately, common implementations of multifactor authentication simply convert the *know + have* pair of secrets into a session token or a browser cookie—just another secret, with all the problems that a secret entails.

Authentication is a hard problem, because it means translating the true identity of an entity—who a person is—into a digital form that doesn't suffer from the same weaknesses as secrets.

Authorization

Once identity is established, authorization determines which actions a subject can perform—for example, read-only access versus full access.

Thinking about authorization, it's easy to see why secrets-based access is inadequate without a strong tie to an identity. Your house key gives you (or anyone who possesses it) the ability to enter your home, but it is your identity that gives you *authorization* to do so. You can grant authorization to others, allowing them to perform specific actions. You might authorize someone to repair a leaky faucet or invite a friend to dinner. Hopefully, you're granting these permissions based on identity rather than possession of a house key.

Authorization is separate from authentication but relies on it. Without knowing who is requesting access to a resource, it's impossible to decide whether to grant access. Authorization consists of policy definition and policy enforcement: deciding who has access to which resources and enforcing those decisions. The matrix of entities and permissions can be very large and complex and has often been simplified by creating access groups and categorizing resources into groups with defined permissions. This simplifies policy management but increases the blast radius of a breach. Someone with a stolen credential gains access to a broad group of resources based on the role to which the credential is assigned.

Audit

Audit shows which actions have been taken by every user or machine and which resources have been affected. The necessity of identifiable audit records—knowing who did what—is another reason why perimeter-based access does not scale. If you rely on a network boundary to authenticate clients, and the resources on an internal network are not protected, it means that all users become merged as a single "guest" (or worse: "admin"), making the audit logs useless.

Once access shifts away from a perimeter-based approach to the resource and application level, generating more detailed and granular events, it becomes even more important to have both a real-time view and a historical record of access. Audit typically falls under the security terminology of manageability and traceability, with the important point being that you actually know and control what is going on in your environment.

Identity-native infrastructure access management provides a great deal of control over individual access privileges, but the flip side of that is the responsibility to ensure that privileges are revoked when they are no longer needed. Regular audits can help minimize the risk of privileges being assigned incorrectly or lingering beyond when they're needed. In other words, auditing is another hedge against human error.

Having a real-time view and a historical record of access is a critical security capability. Shifting away from a perimeter-based approach to identity-native infrastructure access provides a great deal of control over access, because with audits each access can be tied back to an identity at an individual level.

Security Versus Convenience

Security and convenience are famously at odds with each other. When we approach our house after a grocery run, we are forced to slow down, put the bags on the porch, and reach for the keys. This is hardly convenient, especially when it rains!

The inconvenience of security is even more evident in computing environments. Quite often, there are two groups of engineers involved in making decisions about remote access. On the one hand, we have software developers who need to fix bugs quickly, ship new features to customers, improve performance, and troubleshoot abnormalities—all under a tight timeline. On the other hand, there are security and compliance engineers who are primarily concerned with risk.

These two groups have wildly different incentives. Software developers don't want security in the way because it slows them down—and in many cases the way security is measured really has nothing to do with actual security. Security and compliance engineers are more concerned with reducing risk than with how fast things get done. As a result, there's often tension between developers and security engineers, which sometimes takes the form of open conflict. A trade-off needs to be found.

Organizations approach this in a variety of ways. Smaller technology startups err on the side of productivity, because their primary risk is not a security risk but a business risk. They may still be focusing on finding the product market fit, so the speed of product iteration is more important than compliance. As they mature, the balance starts to shift toward more robust security practices and compliance enforcement, trading off some of the product development velocity in the process.

The industry shift to cloud computing has contributed to this dilemma. Engineers have gained more control over their infrastructure because the infrastructure itself is now provisioned with code. Oppressive security processes create incentives for engineers to implement their own shortcuts, which is easy with infrastructure-as-code provisioning. Often, management believes they have adopted solid security measures, while in reality their engineering team has devised its own ways of accessing cloud environments. This approach is called *security theater*.

Therefore, we can conclude that an infrastructure access system is only secure if the engineering team actually loves using it.

Scaling Hardware, Software, and Peopleware

The definition of *infrastructure* is expanding. As remote work and personal devices become part of the workplace, and diverse computing environments proliferate, the surface area of what we once thought of as infrastructure has become impossibly complex. It's no longer practical to think in terms of networks and perimeters. Think of a company like Tesla with a network of charging stations and millions of vehicles around the globe, all of them equipped with numerous CPUs, storage, and connectivity. What do they deploy software updates to? Their deployment target is planet Earth!

As infrastructure expands, we need to realize that it's not homogeneous. There are many different kinds of resources and users, each with different roles, needs, and policies. We need to enforce different behaviors in different contexts: development, staging, test, and production, for example. We need to protect the entire software development supply chain from vulnerabilities (human error), and to limit the blast radius in case of a breach. Managing access securely in all these environments, with so many related goals and moving parts, is immensely complex.

Infrastructure has been able to scale quickly by moving from managing physical devices to using APIs for provisioning virtual devices. Because everything can be defined and managed as code (infrastructure as code [IaC]), it's easy to scale elastically by provisioning more of whatever resource you need. Networks are dynamic and resources are completely fungible. Everything listens on its own network socket and needs access to some number of other resources. Tracking and blocking every network socket and endpoint to prevent infiltration would be impossible.

Ultimately, the difficulty in managing infrastructure access comes from scaling all three major elements of a computing environment:

Hardware
> The physical components that make up the system, including servers, storage, personal computers, phones, and networking devices

Software
> Containers, Kubernetes clusters, databases, monitoring systems, internal web applications, services, and clients that communicate with each other within a VPC or across networks

Peopleware
> The human role in information technology, including software developers, DevOps, and security teams

All three of these elements are growing more complex as they scale. It's common for an organization to have tens of thousands of geographically distributed servers running more and more diverse cloud computing environments that include VMs, containers, Kubernetes clusters, databases, and an army of logging and monitoring tools. This leads to access silos across these dimensions:

- Hardware access is siloed because cloud infrastructure is accessed differently from the older environments colocated in a traditional data center.

- Software access is siloed because databases are accessed via a VPN, Secure Shell (SSH) is accessed via a series of jump hosts with private keys stored in a vault, and CI/CD tools are accessible on a public IP address and hooked to a corporate single sign-on (SSO) system.

- Peopleware access is siloed because some teams use manually provisioned accounts with a password manager to access their systems, others use SSO, and other teams have special requirements—such as a compliance team that allows certain types of access only from an approved laptop stored in a safe.

At the same time, as teams become more distributed and elastic, relying on contractors and other outside contributors, it's necessary to quickly provision, manage, and, importantly, deprovision access.

Figure 1-1 shows how silos inevitably begin to appear at scale. Each piece of software (represented by the shaded rectangles) has its own access method—already a silo. As the infrastructure sprawls to multiple environments, such as Amazon Web Services (AWS) and on-prem, this creates additional silos that are orthogonal to the software silos. As an organization at scale hires elastically, the contractors are likely to be segregated to their own access methods for security reasons. Even worse, different roles are sometimes forced into different access methods. The result is a multidimensional matrix of siloes that make consistent application of access policy all but impossible.

As we automate more and more tasks, the role of a human is supposed to be decreasing with time. To make this work, software needs the ability to communicate securely and autonomously with other software to support automated processes such as CI/CD deployments, monitoring, backups, the interactions of microservices in distributed applications, and dynamic delivery of information. Traditional security methods use tokens, cookies, and other secrets tailored to the growing number of separate tools with slightly different security protocols. This not only doesn't scale but provides no way to track and correct human errors when they lead to vulnerabilities and breaches.

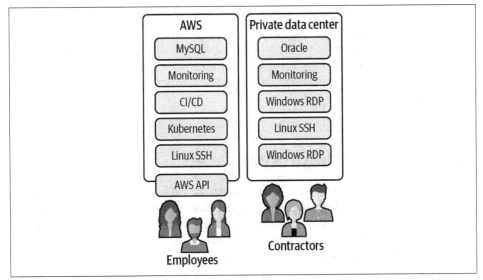

Figure 1-1. How silos emerge as infrastructure scales

In other words, the separation between humans accessing machines and machines accessing each other creates yet another access silo: humans versus machines.

The most vulnerable component in an information system is the peopleware: users, administrators, developers, and others who access the system. Every breach can be traced back to a human error somewhere. The complexity of working with so many different access protocols, with their associated secrets and multifactor authentication procedures, leads people to take shortcuts: remaining logged in between sessions, reusing passwords, writing down secrets, and other bad behaviors. This tendency increases the probability of an exploitable mistake. Often, well-intended new security measures increase drag on the people who use them, leading them to cut corners even more to preserve some level of productivity.

The point is that a growing number of access silos, each with its own secrets, protocols, authentication, and authorization methods, and so on, leads to an unmanageable labyrinth of vulnerabilities that tend to increase as the complexity of access starts to interfere with people's ability to be productive.

To solve the problem, it's necessary to reduce complexity, which will not only improve the user experience but improve security by making it more manageable. While we're at it, to remove the element of human error, it would be beneficial to move away from a secrets-based model of security. But reducing the probability of human error requires more than reducing the number of secrets. It's also necessary to tame the complexity of configuring access for a vast array of different kinds of resources, breaking down silos by bringing hardware, software, and peopleware under a single, unified source of truth for access policy.

Unifying access control across humans, machines, and applications reduces the need for expertise to configure connectivity, authentication, authorization, and audit in all these different systems; reduces complexity overall; and makes consistent auditability possible. Reducing complexity, in turn, gets security out of the way of convenience and productivity, giving engineers fewer reasons to take shortcuts or otherwise undermine security policy.

It turns out that there is an approach that can accomplish these goals.

Identity-Native Infrastructure Access

The whole point of identity-native infrastructure access is to move away from secrets entirely. Secrets are just data, and data is vulnerable to human error. True identity is not data that can be downloaded, copied, or stolen. True identity is a characteristic of the physical world. You are you. The most difficult aspect of granting access based on identity is the problem of representing physical identity digitally. Secrets tied to usernames were a futile attempt to bring user identities into the digital realm.

The idea of using a centralized identity store was the first attempt at reducing the number of secrets within an organization. Instead of each application maintaining its own list of user accounts with accompanying logins and passwords, it makes sense to consolidate all user accounts in one database and have it somehow shared across many applications. That's pretty much how centralized identity management (IdM) systems work. They consolidate user accounts into a single location and offer a standardized API for applications to access them. For example, when a user requests access to a web application, the application redirects the user to an IdM system like Okta or Active Directory. The IdM presents its own login to authenticate the user, transfers a representation of the user's identity back to the user's computer, and redirects the user back to the application they are trying to access, supplied with the user's identity in the form of a token.

Figure 1-2 shows the SSO login sequence top to bottom:

1. An unauthenticated user (no token, no session cookie) tries to access a web app.

2. The web app redirects the user to an IdM such as Active Directory.

3. The user logs into the IdM with their credentials.

4. The IdM sends the user's identity as a token.

5. The user can now gain access to the web app by supplying the authentication token.

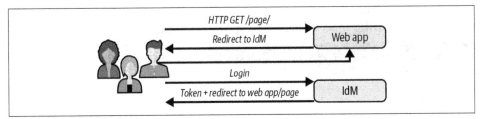

Figure 1-2. The SSO login sequence

It is easy to see why this approach scales better: no matter how many applications or other identity-aware resources an organization deploys, the number of secrets stays the same. Moreover, the overhead of provisioning and deprovisioning access for employees joining or leaving a team remains the same.

While IdM is a big step forward, it does not eliminate secrets entirely; it merely reduces their number. Let's not forget about the browser cookie. Because a cookie is just another secret, it doesn't solve the underlying problem. Steal the cookie and you can become someone else.

Another practical problem with identity management systems is that they were primarily developed with web applications in mind. The common protocols used with IdM are HTTP protocols: Security Assertion Markup Language (SAML), OAuth2, and OpenID Connect. Meanwhile, computing infrastructure relies on much older resource-specific protocols such as SSH, remote desktop protocol (RDP), MySQL, PostgreSQL, and others that do not work in a browser and cannot natively be integrated with an IdM system.

Therefore, the two primary challenges in implementing identity-native infrastructure access are:

- Moving away from storing identity as secret data
- Finding a way to transfer identity using native infrastructure protocols

Moving identity management away from secrets means attaching to a real, physical world identity by using biometric authentication for humans and hardware security modules for machines.

The next question is how to transfer true identity into the digital realm because an access system needs to interact with true identity somehow. The best currently available mechanism to safely transfer true identity into an access system is digital certificates. Table 1-1 shows how certificates compare to secrets as an access control mechanism.

Table 1-1. A comparison of the characteristics of certificates and secrets

	Certificates	Secrets
Standardized across protocols and applications	Yes	No
Vulnerability to theft	Low	High
Management overhead	Low	High
Identity and context metadata	Yes	No

Certificates can be issued to machines, humans, and applications. Certificates are natively supported by common infrastructure protocols. Certificates are safer than secrets because they are far less exposed to theft and misuse. A certificate can be revoked, set to expire automatically, be issued for a single use, and pinned to a specific context (intent) and network address. This makes stealing a certificate nearly pointless. The certificate chain of trust back to a certificate authority (CA) leaves only a single secret to protect—the CA itself—no matter the scale of the organization. In other words, this approach scales forever without compromising security.

A modern, certificate-based central identity management system holds no other secrets besides the CA. True identity of clients is stored not in a database, but in the real world as identifying physical attributes of humans and machines: human biometrics, hardware security modules, and trusted platform modules. The identity transfer is carried in a certificate that can be pinned to a context and limited in time. This brings access effectively into a single plane where all the pillars of access happen uniformly based on every entity's true identity.

This approach is the foundation not only of providing stronger security and more convenient access for users but dealing with challenges of scale and complexity. The approach rests on the two principles mentioned earlier: removing secrets (to eliminate human error) and Zero Trust (to make a pivot impossible if a breach occurs).

This is the approach hyperscale companies have adopted. Moving away from secrets means moving toward digital representation of the true identities of hardware, software, and peopleware. Zero Trust means not just encrypting all connections but designing all infrastructure components to be safe without a firewall—because there's no perimeter.

The following chapters explain how it's done, and why it doesn't have to be painful.

## CHAPTER 2

Identity

Traditionally, infrastructure access has never been identity-based. Instead, it has relied on data *associated with* an identity—mainly in the form of usernames, passwords, private keys, and other secrets—which can be easily compromised, leaving critical systems open to attack. This chapter explores the difference between credentials and identity, the types of identities involved in infrastructure access, and secure forms of credentials that are not vulnerable to human error and, therefore, not prone to leaking.

We begin with your identity. An *identity* is the fact of you being who you are, usually recognized by a unique set of physical attributes that distinguish you from anyone else. These attributes include your face, your fingerprint, your DNA, and other aspects of your physical self. A server, container, applications—anything that exists—has an identity, too. The identity of an infrastructure resource is defined by its physical attributes as well, as we'll cover later in this chapter.

Establishing and proving identity is a tricky problem. It quickly becomes necessary to use *credentials* or claims about the identity of a person or other entity. Various kinds of credentials have been invented to prove identity, and they all have their deficiencies.

At some point, whether at birth or later in your life, you're issued a national identification number such as a Social Security number (SSN).[1] You probably also have a license to operate a motor vehicle, including a photograph of your face, a unique license number, and other information about you. From time to time,

---

[1] Most countries have equivalents: the SIN in Canada, the CPR number in Denmark, and the kojin bangō (個人番号) in Japan, for example.

you've probably used one of these credentials to identify yourself. In fact, these two credentials are very different from each other.

Your SSN is a unique string of digits connected to you. This number was created to track your earnings for the purpose of calculating your retirement benefits. It was never intended to serve as a form of identification. When a business requests your SSN, they generally don't ask to see your Social Security card. An SSN is a single authentication factor. Theoretically, it's no better than a secret, but it's worse because it's not really secret—it's everywhere. Anyone who knows your SSN can use it as a credential. That's a big problem, and has helped drive an epidemic of identity theft, in which one person poses as another to obtain credit cards or engage in other identity-related crime.

Your driver's license is a more secure proxy for your identity. A driver's license provides better proof of identification than your SSN, because it includes your likeness, signature, address, and an expiration date. By matching the photo to your face or comparing your signature in person to the one on the license, anyone can have some degree of confidence that you are the person identified by the driver's license. It also contains a unique ID number. Simply knowing the number is not enough; the license itself must be physically present if you want to use it in the real world—to order a drink in a restaurant in the US where the legal drinking age is 21, for example, or during a traffic stop. This is a critical aspect of identity-native access: *secure forms of identification must never be represented as mere data*; they must be tied to physical objects. Your driver's license can be stolen, but at least it can't be stolen over the internet. And even if it's stolen, the things that tie it to your true identity make it difficult for another person to use.

The difference boils down to one thing: the SSN is merely information you know, while the driver's license is a physical object that also captures who you are: your face, your signature, and other attributes that make you unique. Even so, the driver's license is imperfect. It is not you, and the photograph is not your face.

In other words, *your true identity is not data about you, but the collection of physical attributes of you*. Identity is stored in the physical world, not in the world of ones and zeros. Much of the difficulty in proving identity comes from the challenge of representing identity—who you are—without turning it into data, which is vulnerable to theft. As the next sections reveal, many of the problems of representing identity in the physical world are the same or worse in the digital realm.

Identity and Access Management

Identity and access management, also known as *access control*, is the process of ensuring that only identified, authenticated, authorized entities gain access to protected resources, systems, or services. *Identity proofing*, verifying credentials against actual identity, is the foundation of access control. The ability to establish the identity of every client is also the key to enforcing *role-based access control* (*RBAC*), giving clients access only as needed for the roles they perform.

Consider the problem of managing access to a database. A database account is both an *identification system* and a form of *access control*. It includes features intended to identify clients definitively and designed to be difficult to misuse. A user management system built into a database must do three things when you request access:

Identification
> Establishing who you are

Authentication
> Verifying that you are who you claim to be

Authorization
> Confirming your eligibility to do something

Only if you can be identified, authenticated, and authorized can you gain access to the database. Figure 2-1 shows the relationship between these three aspects of an access control system.

Figure 2-1. The three parts of access control

The first time you request a database account to be provisioned, you have to establish your identity with the database administrators. Consider the possibility of a spoofing attack at this point. Theoretically, someone else could also state your name, claiming to be you, perhaps via a falsified email message. Your name or your email address are just data about your identity, after all, not your identity itself.

To authenticate you, establishing that you are who you say you are, requires additional factors of proof. This concept, called multifactor authentication (MFA), relies on several different kinds of evidence, generally including at least two of the following:

- *Something you know*, such as a username and password
- *Something you have*, a USB device such as YubiKey or a computer equipped with a unique, trusted platform module (TPM)
- *Something you are*, such as a fingerprint or your face

When you got your driver's license for the first time, you had to physically go to the DMV. You probably provided your name, date of birth (something you know) and certified documents such as a birth certificate and a utility bill (something you have). Most importantly, you had to be physically present to have your photo taken (something you are). The DMV, once it was confident it had *established your identity*, was able to issue you a credential: your driver's license.

Identity and Credentials

Credentials are an identity *proxy*—an attempt to convert real identity, which can't be transmitted or shared, into data, which can. An identity proxy is useful, because it makes it possible to share trust, but it's also dangerous: like any data, credentials can be stolen or misused. When people talk about identity theft, what they really mean is the theft of credentials. Since credentials are the normal way of proving identity, credential theft creates huge problems, both in the real and digital world.

True identity can't be stolen or spoofed. There is only one you. Credentials are merely information about you. When someone steals your driver's license or database password, they don't become you, but they might be able to pretend they are you. This difference is the root of all the vulnerabilities related to access control because it gives human error a foothold into identity.

Traditional Approaches to Access

The traditional approach to establishing and using identity in the digital realm is a compromise that attempts to use accounts with secret-based credentials as a transmissible proof of identity. As illustrated in Figure 2-2, to interact with a computing resource, an identity is often linked to an *account*, essentially a database record describing a user or other entity. Each account is configured with a set of roles and permissions that provide appropriate access to resources. An account is a simplistic way of establishing identity because it can be used by any client that can provide a valid credential. An account doesn't really require proof of identity, only possession of the secret associated with the account.

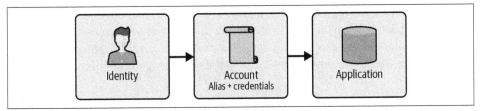

Figure 2-2. How accounts provide access to applications

Still, accounts are a widespread form of identity proxy. In a typical infrastructure environment, a handful of users might be associated with hundreds of login accounts, each configured with multiple roles and privileges. Managing user accounts for every computing resource is time consuming. As an organization grows, provisioning and deprovisioning access becomes harder and synchronizing permissions across different types of resources approaches impossible.

To alleviate this pain, computing resources are often designed to work with accounts in groups, because it makes it possible to redefine access policy rules in batches, making an administrator's job easier. Team members sometimes share team accounts and credentials with each other for simplicity, ease of collaboration, or to save the cost of purchasing additional accounts. Even where administrators are required to manage a secure account life cycle with periodic password rotations for administrative accounts, they may favor sharing a single administrative account with multiple users for convenience instead of creating multiple least-privilege accounts.

When accounts and credentials are shared, it becomes very challenging to track who did what and when. Account-based access, which tends toward this kind of sharing, is fundamentally flawed because it doesn't tie roles and privileges to individuals, making it impossible to audit or trace resource usage or security events. Worse, accounts often rely on secret-based credentials, which have a number of serious problems.

Why secrets are bad

A secret-based credential uses a protected piece of information, such as a password or key, to prove identity. If you know the secret word, you are who you say you are—or so the theory goes.

While secret-based credentials remain popular to the point of predominance, they don't prove identity. Every capability you might want for identity-based access, from building a chain of trust to verifying who really did something, is missing from secrets-based credentials. A secret is just a piece of information, so anyone who holds the secret gains access to whatever it unlocks. This makes secrets an attack point.

Every successful infrastructure attack follows the same human error + pivot pattern. First, an attacker exploits a human error—such as a leaked secret—to establish a foothold. Then the attacker moves laterally, trying to pivot to adjacent systems, increasing the area where the attacker can cause damage, commonly called the *blast radius.*

According to Verizon's 2023 Data Breach Investigations Report (DBIR) (*https://oreil.ly/0-W_l*), the most common attack patterns are compromised credentials, misused credentials, social engineering, and phishing. These patterns all have human error in common. It just so happens that most human errors leading to breaches revolve around secrets. Passwords and other secrets are now considered a liability because they increase the probability of human error.

Meanwhile, the number of resources, and the number or entities requesting access to them, are both growing at an astonishing rate. Servers, applications, and people are all working with more and more microservices, APIs, and data that must be protected from unauthorized access. Employees are connecting their own devices to the corporate network under bring your own device (BYOD) policies, and more and more inanimate objects are joining the Internet of Things (IoT). Accordingly, the security goals for an organization should be centered around reliably identifying every entity—human, machine, or software—and granting minimal, revocable access to the resources that entity needs, during the time access is needed.

You can trust that humans will always be humans, and they can be counted on to eventually make a mistake, no matter how competent they are. Secret management practices, such as frequent rotation of keys and passwords, are somewhat helpful but can't eliminate risk entirely. The more people involved, and the more secrets they rely on, the greater the probability of a human error. Think of the "surface area" of all accounts as an attack surface on which every secret represents a potential hole. At scale, in an enterprise environment, the number of secrets is gigantic. Modern enterprise infrastructure encompasses an astonishing number of entities—users, servers, APIs, applications, and the like—each with its own role, credentials, and needs for access. In these environments, every secret-based credential becomes a potential source of human error.

Encrypting secrets has the appearance of a possible solution, but encryption simply shifts the attack vector from the secret being encrypted to another secret: the decryption key. This is why large-scale internet companies have stopped relying on secrets entirely. Secrets simply do not scale.

The mere presence of a secret-based credential is a vulnerability, regardless of whether it's stored in a vault or any other encrypted form.

Why shared secrets are worse

In the real world, identity can't be shared—it's tied to a single entity. But a password or a private key can be easily shared. This is a huge problem.

Even if no credentials are stolen or compromised, secret-based credentials can be innocently misused. It is a common, albeit insecure, practice to share credentials among team members. For example, the small number of people who have administrative access to a system might all use the same admin username and password. This is quite convenient! As long as everyone on the team remains trustworthy, authorized, and in the same role, "nothing can go wrong."

This pattern is even more common among service accounts and applications when dozens of microservices may be sharing the same database username and password injected into their code.

Unfortunately, shared secrets have some bad side effects:

Meaningful audit becomes impossible.
Shared secrets make it impossible to track or audit the actions of individual entities. This makes everything more difficult to manage, creates compliance headaches, and makes it much more difficult to investigate and solve problems. Because you can't identify individual users who have logged on, you don't know who did what.

Deprovisioning access becomes difficult.
If a member of the administrative team leaves the organization, it must be possible to revoke that person's access individually based on identity. Otherwise, it becomes necessary to change the username and password used in common by everyone on the team—or worse, look the other way and hope that no former employees exploit this gaping security hole.

Granular authorization becomes impossible.
Security best practices require granting the minimal privileges needed for accomplishing a task. With shared secrets, you can't change one person's authorization without affecting the whole team. The choice is either to force everyone to use a new set of credentials, leading to a disruption for the whole team, or to grant excessive privileges to everyone.

If someone on the team leaks, loses, or abuses the credentials, it's worse: you're either stuck with a big security hole, or you have to reissue the credentials and communicate them to everyone. This goes against the principle that a password is supposed to be a *secret*, a piece of information that's intentionally not shared.

Secrets are a vector for human error

Human error is always there. If no one outside your organization has access to your infrastructure, it might seem that secrets plus encryption are enough. Even without a certificate, when you use Secure Sockets Layer (SSL) to access a server, the communication is encrypted. This keeps unauthorized employees from snooping—and on your own local network, you would think that you don't need to worry about man-in-the-middle attacks. However, every secret is a potential failure point. As the number of secrets grows, the probability that human error will cause a failure approaches 100%.

For the reasons previously described, the mere presence of infrastructure secrets, encrypted or not, is now considered a security hole. Passwords, private keys, API keys, session tokens, and even browser cookies are all vulnerabilities exploitable by human error.

Mapping all secrets within your organization's computing infrastructure is the first step in discovering your *attack surface area*. The end goal of identity-based access is to bring the attack surface area exposed by secrets down to zero.

Identity-Based Credentials

The solution is to move away from secrets—in fact, away from all static credentials—toward true identity that uses the physical attributes of humans and machines. In other words, a credential should be derived from identity, not the other way around. When credentials are derived from physical identity and attested by a single trustworthy authority, it makes it possible to validate identities (authenticate) and enforce access policy (authorize) for hardware, software, and people. Only then does it become possible to add and verify the context of access and enforce policies specific to the roles and entitlement of each entity—this is the heart of identity-native infrastructure access.

Identity-native infrastructure access requires a single source of truth: a place to define policy for all four pillars of access—connectivity, authentication, authorization, and audit. During authentication, the identities of hardware, software, and people must be available to a central access control system. Unfortunately, this approach is rare. While most organizations do maintain a directory of employees and an inventory of computing resources, access is often provisioned in silos, resulting in duplicated or incomplete client accounts across various environments or teams. Access silos make it difficult to enforce a coherent policy.

As a result, many organizations struggle with enforcing even basic common sense rules such as "developers must not access production data." If the identities of developers and machines are not stored in one place, it becomes impossible at the moment of authorization to know whether a client is a developer, whether a machine is a part of a production environment, or whether a machine has any data on it. When centralized identity management is implemented, each entity's access is attached to one true identity recognizable across the entire organization. This can only happen with the establishment of a central identity store for humans and machines.

Good credentials, derived from true identity, play an important role in identity-native infrastructure access. These credentials must be able to carry identity "on the wire" without making it vulnerable to human error, leakage, theft, sharing, or copying.

Establishing Trust in Identity

Because true identity can't be transferred, it's necessary to create a proxy in the form of credentials that can be trusted. One approach is to create a *chain of trust*, where every credential leads back to a reliable, authoritative source of truth. This trusted authority must keep data about every credential and the identity it links to and must be able to revoke credentials whenever necessary.

In the process of issuing a driver's license, the DMV is the trusted authority. The chain of trust looks like this:

- Everyone agrees to trust the DMV.
- You must prove your identity in person to the DMV when you apply for a driver's license.
- Your driver's license is linked to your true identity.

Figure 2-3 shows how a trusted authority is central to establishing and managing identity.

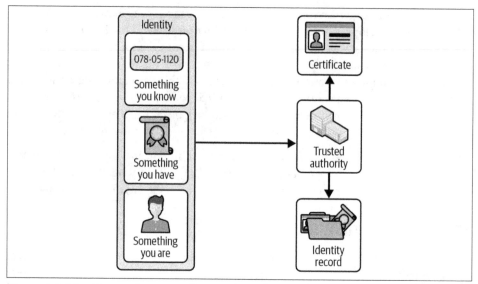

Figure 2-3. Identity proofing, recording, and certification by a trusted authority

When the DMV issues your driver's license, it is giving you a certificate you can use not only to authenticate your identity but prove your authorization to drive a specific class of vehicle: motorcycles, cars, and large trucks require different permissions. This authorization can be upgraded, downgraded, or revoked. The credentials provided by a database administrator have the same function: authentication that you are who you say you are, plus revocable authorization to access the database in specific ways.

If you alter the information on the driver's license, it no longer matches the DMV record of your identity, and the license becomes invalid. If you abuse your database privileges, they can be revoked. The ability to grant and remove authorization is central to establishing trust.

The problem of establishing a chain of trusted identity is not limited to the physical world. Just as you need a way to trust strangers with whom you perform transactions, computing resources, applications, and DevOps engineers need a way to trust each other. A digital certificate helps solve this problem, and is like a driver's license in a number of ways:

- Issued by a trusted authority
- Must be presented during authentication and authorization
- Revocable, and expires periodically
- Linked to identity

Unlike a secret-based credential, a digital certificate provides a way to attest to an individual's identity whether that individual is a person, a server, an application, or some other entity. Certificates provide not only a mechanism for establishing identity, but mechanisms for granting and revoking specific authorizations and policies. The authority that issues a certificate is responsible for issuing credentials, monitoring to detect malicious misuse of trust, and helping to thwart such attempts.

Because certificates expire, they offer additional protection against misuse. When all else fails, a certificate that's been compromised in some way will stop working at some point. By setting aggressively short expiration dates, an organization can use certificates to protect themselves against unauthorized access. Digital certificates issued by a centralized certificate authority (CA) have another important property: the CA becomes a single source of truth for both authentication and authorization for all types of computing resources within an organization, especially when every certificate can be tied to an audit log.

Establishing trust with identity certification is the first step, but organizations must also continuously monitor the security health of devices and networks using a contextual verification modal such as Zero Trust. Chapter 5 discusses these methods.

Identities in Infrastructure

Establishing true identity based on the physical properties of humans and machines is the first and most important step in the access management process. The next major challenge in modern cloud infrastructure is identity and access management at scale. Gone are the days when a small number of people needed access to a few computer programs running on a single system. A typical environment, which now extends to the cloud, consists of thousands of servers, each running thousands of applications that can be accessed by thousands of engineers. These machines, programs, and people must all be securely and reliably identified and given access only to the services and resources they have permission to use.

For true identity-native infrastructure access, it must be possible for any two entities of any type to establish each other's identity and enforce the appropriate access policies without being vulnerable to identity spoofing. Applications and services must be restricted to only the datasets they need, and prevented from accessing others, based on their roles and functions. A server might be in a production environment, with tight controls around data and access, or in a development sandbox where anything goes.

As explored earlier in this chapter, people's true identities reside in the real world. But what about the true identities of machines such as servers, desktops, and laptops?

When you access a Linux server for the first time with a password or key-based authentication, OpenSSH warns you of the server's identity and asks if you're willing to proceed (as you will see later in Figure 2-4). If you can't—or merely don't—verify this key, you have no way of knowing whether the server is genuine or has been planted by an attacker. This problem is called *trust on first use* (*TOFU*). Without verifying the server identity, it's hard to trust the OpenSSH server you are connecting to. The importance of identity in establishing trust can't be overstated (see Example 2-1).

Example 2-1. OpenSSH warning (trust on first use)

```
user@example ~ % ssh root@192.168.1.1
The authenticity of host '192.168.1.1 (192.168.1.1)' can't be established.
ED25519 key fingerprint is SHA256:bFBLXMrkd5fU4Qz+SB9u98oLRozzqIAbMuDGXGA95f8.
This key is not known by any other names
Are you sure you want to continue connecting (yes/no/[fingerprint])?
```

All entities in infrastructure—hardware, software, and peopleware—can operate in many different roles. For example, a human might be a user, developer, administrator, or operations engineer. Similarly, a single server can host and serve multiple different applications. Traditionally, hardware identity has been handled at the network level, tracking every computer by the unique combination of the media access control (MAC) address of its network card, an IP address, and a hostname.

Since the advent of virtual machines (VMs) and software-defined networking (SDN), a single server can now host multiple operating systems, making it harder to track the true identity of a service running inside the server. With container technology, a single operating system can now host multiple services, further masking the true physical identity of the server. The rise of containers has led to managing infrastructure as code (IaC). In this approach, containers and VMs can be *ephemeral*, meaning they exist transitionally as needed, and their identities don't persist.

Let's compare the two different types of identity: long-lived identity and ephemeral identity.

Long-Lived Identities

Long-lived identities are the type we're used to: they're rooted in the physical world and can't be updated or copied easily. Because they're static, long-lived identities are more dependable and easier for use in access control. We can certify a long-lived identity once and use it as long as it meets certain constraints.

People's identities are long-lived and static. Our biological traits remain the same, no matter how old we grow. Similarly, hardware devices have attributes such as serial numbers and manufacturing numbers that are mostly static throughout their lives.

On the internet, the Domain Name System (DNS) assigns a static address for web applications. Corresponding Secure Sockets Layer/Transport Layer Security (SSL/TLS) certificates can be obtained from a trusted third party certifying entity and asserting further trust in the domain name. It doesn't matter if there are changes to the underlying network addresses, hardware, or operating systems that host these web applications. As long as the domain properties remain intact, the domain names and the certificate remain the same. It's these static properties that give us trust while connecting to a website.

The question is how to make these static identities dependable enough. Hardware and its serial numbers can be stolen, and software identities can be spoofed. Even people's apparent identities can change. For example, using plastic surgery, people can change the way they look or even update their biological traits to drop a previous identity, just like in the movies. On a more mundane level, a valid question to ask as we head into a future of biometrics-based identity verification is this: What happens if someone steals my fingerprint from a biometric device?

A huge security risk in long-lived identities is that we also tend to assign long-lived static credentials to these identities. By nature, we humans need some external push before we make a change. If a website doesn't require it, the user may never update their password. It's the same with every other kind of infrastructure access. Engineers will probably never update credentials if not mandated to do so—not even their credentials for the primary server and databases that the whole business depends upon. In other words, the tendency is to rely on the worst security combination: the long-lived identity paired with long-lived, secret-based credentials.

Long-lived identities must always be tied to the physical world, to eliminate the vulnerability that always accompanies secrets.

Ephemeral Identities

Ephemeral identities are by definition short-lived. Ephemeral identities are a byproduct of modern infrastructure management patterns: running cloud native infrastructure with immutable and ephemeral resources. For these resources that don't have a physical presence, even their ephemeral identities must be tied back to a physical, long-lived identity through a chain of trust.

All other things being equal, an ephemeral entity is more secure than a long-lived entity in some ways. If an ephemeral entity is compromised, it has the courtesy to disappear after a while, removing the threat. The DIE triad (Distributed, Immutable, and Ephemeral) is one of the best approaches modern infrastructure has to offer in terms of the next-generation security model.

A physical server, on the other hand, hangs around for a long time and can become a long-standing point of vulnerability if it's compromised. One of the biggest security threats has always been the advanced persistent threat (APT), which can linger for many years inside a compromised network, posing as a trusted identity.

But ephemeral identities come with a catch: How do we securely assign credentials to something that is short-lived? The security that a short lifetime brings to an ephemeral identity is less effective if a team ends up baking in static credentials such as shared secrets or long-lived tokens for convenience.

Ultimately, ephemeral identities and their credentials should be tied back to the true identities of users or machines through a secure chain of identities and trust.

Identity-Native Access

Identity-native access does not rely on secret data but uses the physical properties of hardware and biological attributes of humans instead. This drops the probability of human error in access management to zero. If every party in the access transaction has a way of asserting its true identity, then policy can be enforced without the need for secrets, opening up a secure way to ensure that only authorized entities have appropriate access to protected resources.

In the context of identity-native infrastructure access, every access request made by clients or services must be accounted for and attributed to real-world identity and authorization, without identities or credentials being vulnerable to human error, theft, or spoofing. Identity-native infrastructure access requires a better way to carry the physical world identity into the digital domain *without representing identity as data*. The combination of digital certificates, metadata, and a chain of trust is part of the answer. We'll start with the storage of identity itself.

Identity Storage

To implement identity-native access to infrastructure in the modern, cloud native, and highly elastic world means definitively identifying hardware, software, and peopleware. Of these three, the identity of hardware is arguably most important because it is the foundation of all identity proxy throughout infrastructure.

To provide machine identity, cryptographic storage systems like hardware security modules (HSMs) and Trusted Platform Modules (TPMs) provide secure identity storage across a variety of computing devices such as servers, desktops, and laptops.

TPMs and HSMs are similar to each other. Each of these technologies contains a microchip that stores a unique private key for the machine. The key is inaccessible for reading by software. Instead, HSMs and TPMs only offer signing, verification, and sometimes encryption capabilities. This makes TPMs and HSMs similar to human fingerprints. They can verify machine identity, but there is no data to be stolen: the machine key is "baked" into the hardware and not accessible via any kind of an API. Some of these devices are even tamperproof, making it difficult or impossible to extract the key even if the device itself is stolen. This technology is available not just for physical hardware, but for virtual computing resources.

The public cloud providers offer virtualized HSM services for them, such as NitroTPM or CloudHSM, both on Amazon Web Services (AWS).

The important principle that connects HSMs, TPMs, and human fingerprints is that *true identity is stored in the physical world*. None of the data making up an identity is accessible by a bash script, and none of it can be collected in a database. The obvious benefit is that true identity is never accessible for an attacker to steal or for an employee to accidentally leak.

Organizations ultimately can't get away from some need to store identity digitally as data. Every company has a database of employees, their titles and roles, the laptops and other assets assigned to them, and an inventory of physical servers, Kubernetes clusters, or virtual instances in their cloud environments. To manage identity and authorization securely, these databases and inventories must contain only the relationships between identities, but not the identities themselves. The representation of each entity's identity is stored elsewhere, more securely. For example, the private key of a machine is stored on its HSM, and only the public key is allowed to be stored in a database. An engineer's fingerprint is stored on their laptop's TPM where it can't be read, but the TPM can produce a hash of a fingerprint signed by its private key, and that information can be stored in a database.

When access is granted on the basis of true identity, information about the relationships and roles of identities becomes less sensitive. This secondary information, no longer used as credentials, doesn't grant access and doesn't need to be secret.

Identity Attestation

Identity-native infrastructure access can only work if identity can be proven reliably. There must be a trusted party who can digitally attest to the identities of hardware, software, and peopleware. Practices such as device attestation and using TPMs and HSMs enable secure hardware identification. Similarly, an identity for each employee is established during onboarding, where biometric information is registered with the identity management system acting as a single source of truth for peopleware identification.

This lays the groundwork for separating identity from credentials.

Credentials at scale

Credentials must also operate at scale, which means every credential must be pinned to physical identity and to usage context, so it cannot be reused elsewhere at a different time by a different party. This enables scale, because the probability of an error does not increase with the number of the current credentials in a computing environment. Stealing such credentials brings no benefit to an attacker.

To scale access management along with the speed of infrastructure growth, access and credential management must be automated, resource efficient, and low latency. This requires identity-based, scalable, stateless credentials. A digital certificate can work as that kind of credential.

How digital certificates work as credentials

Both long-lived and ephemeral entities need to be able to represent their identities safely in the digital realm, in a way that's traceable back to the true, long-lived identity of a user or machine based on a chain of identity and trust. Certificates provide a way to attest to identity, accompanied by metadata that ties identity to authorization and policy. Because certificates can expire as quickly as necessary, they also minimize the time window during which they can be compromised. These attributes make certificates a very attractive type of credential.

A certificate provides important features for authenticating and authorizing a client. A certificate:

- Contains unique identifying information about a client
- Has an expiration date and can be revoked
- Can prove its authenticity
- Is issued by a trusted third party (CA)
- Can be pinned to context (network address, client device, and time window)

Certificates reduce the probability of human errors: they are ephemeral, they're tied to a specific device, they are not valuable outside of their usage context and, therefore, they are not a valuable attack target.

A certificate can also contain client permissions, whether the certificate holder is a person, a machine, an application, or something else. This eliminates access silos and makes it possible to enforce policies such as preventing developers from touching production data. The server doesn't have to know if it is part of the staging or production environment, whether it has any data on it, or whether the client is a developer or not. But if the server, the database software, and the client all have certificates with the appropriate metadata, then access can be granted or denied just by examining the certificates of the parties involved. This access can be granted for extremely short periods of time, ad hoc if necessary.

A certificate is the best technology we have to solve the issue of representing physical world identity with data. Certificates make it possible for every access request to be accounted for and attributed to real-world identity and authorization, without the client's identity or credentials being vulnerable to human error, theft, or spoofing. Certificates provide several benefits:

Identity attestation
Upon identity verification, a CA can issue certificates to people, issue certificates to software using a code/application signing process, or issue certificates to hardware based on the keys in their hardware security modules.

Centralized identity management
No matter which department an employee or service belongs to, the CA hierarchy allows distributing sub-CAs that can be configured specifically to a particular department/team's requirements, enabling centralized identity management.

Credential derived from identity
Certificates are attested identity-based credentials signed by the CA. After initial authentication, the server can issue session credentials derived from the certificate—meaning that even the ephemeral credential is derived from the true identity of the person or the machine requesting access. Certificates cannot be shared and are useless without the client's private key and their biometrics that are protected by hardware.

Easy and automatic revocation of the credential
A certificate has an expiration date that automatically invalidates it after a set period of time. Further, the certificate infrastructure maintains a certificate revocation list that can be used to invalidate a certificate prior to its expiration time.

Tamperproof credentials
During the certificate signing process, the CA calculates the hash of the certificate metadata and cryptographically signs it with the CA's private key. This means all the properties of certificates, including the metadata that contains client's roles and permissions, are tamper resistant because any changes would result in a different hash value.

Credential scalability
Certificates are supported by all services and are common protocols used in infrastructure management, which means the same certificate-signing process can scale to an arbitrary number of clients and resources. The entire process can be automated and the total number of secrets present in your organization doesn't grow with the infrastructure.

How certificates are created

In a typical access control scenario, a certificate is created in four steps:

1. The organization sets up a central trusted entity, the CA. A CA is just a private key.
2. The client generates its own private key.
3. The client generates a public key derived from its private key.
4. The client establishes its identity in an onboarding process, registering with the CA by supplying its own public key.

In public key infrastructure (PKI) terminology, this last step is known as the certificate signing request (CSR). The process may require clients to perform out-of-band (OOB) identity verification. This is similar to identity verification during someone's first DMV visit. The CA signs the client's public key with the CA's own private key. The result is a certificate: the client's public key, combined with a time to live (TTL) timestamp and additional metadata about the client, signed by the CA's private key. The certificate (shown in Figure 2-4) can only be useful on the client whose HSM stores the corresponding private key, and only until its TTL expires.

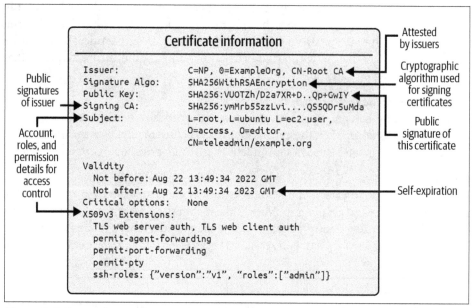

Figure 2-4. Parts of a certificate

Reducing the Number of Secrets to One

Throughout this chapter, we have discussed the risk of secret-based credentials and how this risk has been exponentially increased in modern infrastructure management. Digital certificates address many issues related to identity verification based on secret-based credentials but aren't entirely secretless themselves.

Certificates are based on public-key cryptography. The security of public-key cryptography depends on the secrecy of the private key. The significance of a compromised private key can be similar to a stolen password. Therefore, the private keys of clients should only be stored in memory or—even better—within a secure enclave such as a HSM or a TPM.

Usage of enclaves keeps the private key inaccessible by anyone, including the client itself. When used this way, client or host certificates become completely immune to theft, and the number of client private keys needing management will be zero regardless of how many clients or hosts you may have.

In modern PKI, certificates are based on a chain of trust. All the end user and machine certificates are issued and signed ultimately by the root CA, as illustrated in Figure 2-5. In a typical organization, there may be thousands of certificates, but there will be only one root CA. As long as the root CA private key is protected, we can methodically contain the impact of subsequent certificate compromises.

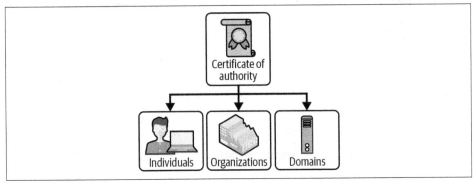

Figure 2-5. The root CA signs and issues certificates to every resource

This is a great improvement over reliance on thousands of passwords and other secrets. Since every certificate is just a signed ephemeral key pair in the chain of trust, an organization that uses PKI only has a single static secret to protect: the root CA.

It is worth noting that management of certificate authorities is similar to management of any other secrets. It's especially important to periodically rotate CAs. At the same time, protecting a single key is easier and more reliable than protecting a thousand keys.

A Path to Identity-Native Infrastructure Access

As we have discussed in this chapter, true identity is the core of access control because it allows us to move away from secrets. Secrets make identification, authentication, authorization, and audit vulnerable to human error. The last sections sum up the most important tactics for moving infrastructure access toward identity-native access.

Eliminate Access Silos

Centralized identity management has seen great progress in internal applications, especially web application access via the use of single sign-on (SSO) solutions. But in most organizations, there is an identity gap between corporate directory management systems and the infrastructure resources hosted on cloud or cloud native environments. With cloud solutions being introduced at a rapid pace, teams operating huge enterprise IT environments struggle to keep up with an explosion of access requirements, creating access silos across different computing environments. For organizations that started their infrastructure operations in traditional data centers, the expansion to the cloud introduces even more access silos. The good news is that identity-native access relies on open standards commonly supported by traditional and cloud native workloads.

To make consolidating identity easier, prioritize procuring software that offers bring your own identity (BYOI) integration. Infrastructure tooling built with BYOI in mind natively supports identity management, making it easier to consolidate identity in a single source of truth for access.

Finally, consider implementing a unified access control system. Unified access control systems automate PKI management and create a common layer between all the infrastructure resources and existing corporate identities. They unify authentication, authorization, and audit for all infrastructure components. This makes it easy to integrate a centralized certificate authority and certificate-based access on top of what you already have, breaking silos without making drastic changes to your current infrastructure operations.

Move to Certificates for Identity Proofing

The next iteration for identity proofing is to become completely passwordless. The industry standard that facilitates passwordless authentication (FIDO2 WebAuthn) is based on public-key cryptography.

Digital certificates offer security and flexibility, making them the closest digital replica of the personal credentials we have in the real world. Passwordless authentication for linking the biometric material of a human to a private key on their device TPM, and issuing a short-lived certificate based on that combination, is currently the most secure available technology for identity proofing. Investing in PKI infrastructure and client devices with hardware security modules is the first step toward implementing identity-native infrastructure access.

Extend Identity-Native Access to Service Accounts

In modern infrastructure operations, service accounts and bots probably access infrastructure resources more frequently than people do. Service accounts, CI/CD tools, and other infrastructure automation have been prime attack targets, as they often have privileged access to critical infrastructure resources. The separation of humans and machines represents another access silo, leading to vulnerability through management complexity. To help solve this problem, teams should tie credentials to identity for machines and bots, just as they do for users.

## CHAPTER 3

Secure Connectivity

Networks no longer play a role in access control in general. While secure, efficient, scalable connectivity is the backbone of computing infrastructure, the network perimeter is no longer in charge. All subjects and objects, clients and resources—all hardware, software, and peopleware—must be able to communicate securely over untrusted networks regardless of their location. This is *Zero Trust access*, an important foundation for identity-based infrastructure access.

This chapter reviews patterns and techniques for modern connectivity management and lays the foundation for a set of practices that don't rely on a network to provide security. Zero Trust is an important part of identity-native infrastructure access because it prevents an attacker from pivoting from one compromised system to the next. The identity-native approach routes all connectivity through Identity-Aware Proxies (IAPs) that permit only authenticated and encrypted connections.

Before we move further into this book, it is important to revisit the basic principles of cryptography, as cryptography is at the core of every technology that enables us to properly implement identity-native infrastructure access.

Cryptography

Securing communications with cryptography is not a new scheme. As far back as the time of Julius Caesar, substitution ciphers were used to conceal secret messages. Cryptography became important in World War I, as the invention of radio made it possible to transmit strategic messages more quickly—an early form of networked communication. Interest in cryptography blossomed further during World War II, when the German military transmitted secret messages using an encryption device called the Enigma machine, whose code was famously deciphered by Polish mathematicians.

The emergence of computer networks and their infiltration into nearly every aspect of our lives has brought encryption out of the military realm, making it something civilians now use every day. Modern encryption methods are more sophisticated, but many of them have some things in common with even the oldest types of encryption. We still use algorithms and keys. In fact, one way of classifying encryption algorithms is by the number of keys they use:

- Hash functions perform one-way encryption and have no decryption key.
- Symmetric encryption uses one key for encryption and decryption.
- Asymmetric encryption uses one key for encryption and another for decryption.

One-Way Functions and Hashing

One-way functions take an input and transform it, generating output that is extremely hard, or even impossible, to reverse and determine what the original input value was.

Hashing is a popular example of a one-way function. In essence, a hash function takes a message or piece of data and computes a short, fixed-length string called a *digest* (also commonly known as a *checksum* or *fingerprint*). An input, when processed through a chosen algorithm, always produces the same digest; the result can be used for integrity checks or simply identifying and comparing blobs of data. Hashing functions are essential to security because they make it possible to verify messages and passwords relatively securely. Hashing functions are a fundamental building block of numerous network encryption protocols including SSH, Internet Protocol Security (IPsec), TLS, and others. We'll cover some security-related uses of hashing in the section, "Authenticated encryption with associated data (AEAD)" on page 40 in this chapter.

There are a number of hashing functions demonstrating different levels of security. Two common hashing functions in use today are the MD (message digest) and SHA (Secure Hash Algorithm) families.

MD is faster than SHA, but the latest version (MD5) has been compromised. That is, it's possible for an attacker to use brute force to find the original message represented by an MD5 digest. Because of its speed, MD5 is useful for low-security tasks like checking that files are not accidentally corrupted, but MD5 should not be used for security purposes.

SHA is much more interesting in the context of cryptography and message security. SHA algorithms have much more *digest uniqueness* than MD algorithms, meaning that the likelihood of any two messages sharing a digest is much smaller. This makes it more difficult to crack than MD algorithms.

There are several hashing functions in the SHA family that differ by the bit length of their output: SHA-1, SHA-2, etc. At the time of this writing, only SHA-2 and SHA-3 are considered to be sufficiently secure, because the economic cost of brute-forcing SHA-1 hashes has been gradually getting lower.

Most Unix-derived systems have a built-in tool for hashing files and strings. For example, the following example shows using the `shasum` command to generate a digest for two different strings using the 256-bit algorithm variant of SHA-2:

```
$ echo -n "The quick brown fox jumps over the lazy dog" | shasum -a 256
d7a8fbb307d7809469ca9abcb0082e4f8d5651e46d3cdb762d02d0bf37c9e592  -
$ echo -n "hello world" | shasum -a 256
b94d27b9934d3e08a52e52d7da7dabfac484efe37a5380ee9088f7ace2efcde9-
```

As you can see, even though the input is two different strings of different lengths, the output length is the same: 256 bits. The entire book *To Kill a Mockingbird* can be fed into the SHA-256 hashing function, and the resulting hash will still be 256 bits.

Symmetric Encryption

Symmetric encryption, also known as secret key cryptography, uses the same key for both encryption and decryption. Encrypting plain text protocols, encrypting blobs of data, and most of the encryption you find on the internet in bulk is handled by symmetric encryption.

Symmetric key cryptography generally falls into two types:

Stream cipher
   This cipher encrypts streaming data byte by byte at a time.

Block cipher
   This cipher encrypts whole blocks at a time.

Stream cipher

In a stream cipher, every bit or byte of the plain-text data or message is encrypted one at a time. Stream ciphers, as the name suggests, are a popular choice for encrypting continuous data streams. For example, streaming network connections and remote access protocols are efficiently encrypted using stream ciphers as encryption and decryption can happen without the need to wait for each whole block of data.

RC4 used to be the most widely adopted stream cipher, supported in TLS, SSL, and SSH protocols. Unfortunately, it suffers from numerous security vulnerabilities, including CVE-2013-0169 (the Lucky 13 attack) that allows a rogue party to carry out a man-in-the-middle (MITM) attack and recover plain-text data, and

CVE-2015-2808[1] that allows a rogue party to recover plain text by just sniffing the network traffic.

The ChaCha family of stream ciphers (a variant of the Salsa20) is the new recommended stream cipher. ChaCha20 is also the default cipher suite in the newer version of OpenSSH.

Block cipher

A block cipher takes blocks of the plain text of a fixed size and encrypts them into blocks of ciphertext, usually the same size as the input plain-text blocks. If a block of plain text is smaller than the fixed size, bits are added to the end to "pad" it to the correct size. Block ciphers are most commonly used for encrypting data at rest.

Advanced Encryption Standard (AES), also known as Rijndael, is the most popular symmetric encryption algorithm. For encryption and decryption, it processes data blocks of 128 bits at a time using key lengths varying from 128, 192, or 256 bits. AES has been adopted by the US government, and AES-256 implementation is considered a golden standard for block ciphers, providing the strongest level of encryption.

Authenticated encryption with associated data (AEAD)

AEAD algorithms perform encryption as well as authenticated hashing, ensuring both the confidentiality and authenticity of encrypted data. We mentioned earlier that hash functions like SHA could be used for integrity checks. But a normal hash function such as SHA alone does not involve any secret keys and therefore can only generate a digest but not encryption. Even though its digest is unique, it does not offer any authenticity, as a rogue party can perform an MITM attack and modify both the data and its digest.

A special type of hashing algorithm, also known as message authentication code (MAC), is used to create an authenticated digest. MAC algorithms work by using the same key for creating a digest that is also used for encryption, creating a direct association between encrypted data and the message digest. In practice, most programs use stream or block ciphers in authenticated mode. The cipher suites with AEAD mode are usually represented as TLS_AES_256_GCM_SHA384 (used in TLS v1.3), ChaCha20-Poly1305 (used in OpenSSH).

Symmetric encryption can encrypt large amounts of data rapidly with very few computational resources. This property makes symmetric encryption algorithms useful for any type of data that requires fast, bulk operation. Symmetric encryption is

---

1 CVE, or Common Vulnerabilities and Exposures, is a system to identify, define and catalog publicly disclosed security vulnerabilities. It was created by MITRE, a not-for-profit organization, and is recognized by the cybersecurity industry to track vulnerabilities. See their CVE website (*https://cve.mitre.org/*) for more information.

also very secure, so long as no unauthorized parties have the key. That is the main weakness of symmetric encryption: the parties need to securely exchange a secret—the key—before they can begin communicating privately. There is always a risk that the key will be intercepted or stolen.

To summarize, symmetric encryption is fast, cheap, and secure if the right hashing functions and ciphers are chosen. But symmetric encryption suffers from poor scalability, namely the need to distribute the same key across all authorized parties, which makes it increasingly vulnerable to human error.

Asymmetric Encryption

Asymmetric encryption, also known as *public-key cryptography* (PKC), uses two different keys: one for encryption and another for decryption.

One of these keys is private and must never be shared with anybody. The other key is called the public key. It can be safely shared with the entire world, even published on a public web page. A public key is generated from the private key using a one-way function called a *trapdoor* function. The major advantage of this added complexity is that it removes the need to share a primary encryption key (i.e., the private key).

To send a message to someone, you can encrypt it with their published public key, which is freely available to anyone. The message can only be decrypted by the owner of the private key, which is a closely guarded secret.

There are two benefits that asymmetric encryption brings over symmetric encryption:

Removes the need for secret sharing
    A message encrypted with a public key can only be decrypted with the corresponding private key. The private key remains secret and is never shared.

Supports digital signatures
    Asymmetric cryptography can be used not only for encryption, but also to validate authenticity of data. Any data digitally signed by a private key can be verified with the corresponding public key.

The RSA algorithm, short for Rivest–Shamir–Adleman (named after the three inventors of RSA), is the de facto standard for asymmetric cryptography. The RSA algorithm is based on the difficulty of factoring large prime numbers and depends on the security of a one-way trapdoor function that is easy to compute in one direction but hard to compute in reverse. RSA keys are much longer than symmetric keys because the keys are involved in making it hard to reverse the trapdoor function: the recommended sizes are at least 2,048 bits. Compare that with AES keys, where 256 bits is considered the safest size.

The larger key size makes encryption and decryption slower, requiring more computational power. Another restriction of RSA is that the length of the plain-text data cannot exceed the length of the key.

Both of these restrictions make asymmetric encryption a poor fit for encrypting large data sets: the algorithm is slower to encrypt, and the encrypted data size is larger when compared with symmetric encryption. This also makes RSA a poor choice for real-time encryption on low-powered devices.

One may conclude that these limitations make RSA impractical, but nothing could be further from the truth. Asymmetric encryption is often used in protocols such as TLS or SSH only to initiate a secure connection, also often known as a handshake. Once an encrypted connection is established, a symmetric encryption algorithm and a symmetric key can be negotiated between two parties and a much more efficient symmetric encryption takes over.

While RSA is still a robust choice, most modern asymmetric encryption implementations now use elliptic-curve cryptography (ECC), due to its greater efficiency with smaller keys, faster key generation and cryptographic operations.

Public-private key pairs

Asymmetric cryptography is based on computationally hard mathematical problems. RSA is based on factoring of prime numbers; ECC is based on discrete logarithms. In both cases, the mathematical problem is used to create the public key from the private key.

The following OpenSSL commands generate a keypair using RSA-2048 bits:

```
$ openssl genrsa -out privatekey.pem 2048
# deduce public key from key pair
$ openssl rsa -in privatekey.pem -outform PEM -pubout -out publickey.pem
```

In the above OpenSSL commands, you can see how to derive a public key from a private key. Public keys are not only safe to publish for everyone to see, but they can also be lost and regenerated again.

Key exchange

Symmetric encryption requires a single encryption key to be exchanged between two parties. To facilitate this, asymmetric encryption is used to implement the key exchange algorithms that many secure network protocols depend on.

Key exchange algorithms enable secure sharing of an encryption key between two different parties without revealing the key at any point in the transaction. The Diffie–Hellman algorithm, one of the first major implementations of public-key cryptography, is still a popular choice for key exchange. Diffie–Hellman is similar to RSA, except in the Diffie–Hellman algorithm, the two communicating parties do not need to share the public key ahead of time. Instead, both parties exchange mathematical modulo challenges and deduce a shared secret key at the end. Diffie–Hellman offers *perfect forward secrecy*, a system that changes keys frequently, which is not possible with plain RSA-based key exchange. In cryptography, perfect forward secrecy is achieved when even the compromise of a private key cannot be used to deduce a session key and decrypt the ciphertext.

Diffie–Hellman does not support digital signatures, which means that it has no mechanism to ensure the authenticity of the data exchanged during the key exchange process. This is why, in practice, the Diffie–Hellman algorithm is used along with RSA or ECC (generally denoted as RSA + DH and ECDH, respectively), offering both authenticity and perfect forward secrecy for the key exchange. The next section discusses digital signatures, another significant application of asymmetric cryptography.

Digital signatures and document signing

A digital signature, like a physical signature, is intended to be easy for someone to create, but difficult for someone else to forge. In a digital signature scheme, there are two algorithms:

Signing algorithm
   This uses a private key to create a message digest or to encrypt the message.

Verification algorithm
   This uses the corresponding public key to check the signature.

Because the encryption performed with the private key can only be decrypted with the corresponding public key, the digital signature provides assurance that the message is authentic. Digital signatures can be used to sign any form of digital data, including documents, network traffic, and program binaries.

Asymmetric cryptography solves the problem of secure key exchange that persists in symmetric cryptography. But as the number of involved parties increases, it becomes cumbersome and error-prone to distribute and update public keys with everyone involved in public-key transactions. Additionally, although the public key lets us verify that the signer holds the private key, how can we ensure that the private key holder is the person they claim to be?

This is where digital certificates come in: they solve the issue of public-key distribution at scale, and also increase trust in the form of attestation.

Certificates as Public Keys

While asymmetric cryptography safely solves the key distribution problem that plagued symmetric crypto for years, it still presents significant operational overhead for publishing and distributing public keys. Using SSH as an example, when an engineer joins a company, their public key must be uploaded to all the servers in scope of access. When a new server comes online, its public key needs to be shared with everyone who needs secure access to it. Every engineer has a list of public keys for all servers stored in their ~/.ssh/known_hosts file, and every machine needs to have a list of all engineers' public keys in ~/.ssh/authorized_keys files for every user. When an engineer leaves the company or a server is decommissioned, the process must be reversed. Certificates simplify management of credentials by getting rid of public keys completely. Let's examine how they work, continuing to use SSH as an example.

An implementation of a certificate-based system begins by generating a private key. This key will play a very important role and will be called a certificate authority (CA). A corresponding public key is also derived from it and published for all to see.

When an engineer joins a team, they generate their own private key, and they send the corresponding public key to someone (or something) who manages the CA. The full name of an engineer, along with other identity-related information such as their roles and other metadata is added to the public key and the whole is signed using the CA private key. The resulting certificate is returned to the engineer and can now be used to access all SSH servers that trust the public key of the CA.

A certificate is just a public key signed by a trusted authority, with metadata describing certain properties of the public key holder and an expiration date. Because a certificate is digitally signed by a CA, it cannot be tampered with. Validating a certificate is easy and safe, because the public key of the issuing CA is published.

Certificates combine all the security bits and pieces that asymmetric cryptography has to offer into one elegant solution:

- Certificates are linked to the identity of their owner based on a digital signature signed by a CA.
- A certificate is just a public-private keypair that can be utilized to establish not only authentication but also encryption.
- A certificate can expire after a specified amount of time.

Certificates also support extensions like custom metadata that can contain access policies, user roles, and other properties.

Certificates facilitate secure key exchange and encryption without the need to share the encryption keys ahead of time. With certificates, you only need to trust the CA. This means certificates relieve the key distribution problems associated with encryption based on plain public-private key pairs. Lastly, the support for digital signatures and trusted issuers means that certificates can scale easily along with cloud native infrastructure.

The Untrusted Network

Traditionally, information security and infrastructure access has been closely associated with networks. Even in the movies, hacking attacks have often been described as "bad guys who infiltrated our networks."

Modern networks are often abstracted at the platform level via software-defined networking. All public cloud providers allow engineers to provision and configure network connectivity via APIs. As the broader infrastructure operations "shift left" toward engineers (DevOps), the rise of everything-as-code means that infrastructure security will follow this trend.

This gives us the opportunity to move security away from the network boundary and closer to workloads, allowing us to identify and authenticate connection to the original client at a highly granular level.

Moreover, there is no longer a traditional "perimeter." With engineers working out of several offices or even their own homes, each with its own local network, connecting to computing resources running across multiple cloud providers, it no longer makes sense to segregate tenants based on network affinity. There is no longer a local area network (LAN) or wide area network (WAN), only clients and resources who by default must never trust each other. Therefore, modern security requirements have outgrown old network-based security techniques based on the notion of a perimeter or traffic segmentation. Networks are just too "dumb" to understand the complexity of the workloads that rely on them. Present-day security threats exploit human errors such as programmer mistakes that lead to vulnerabilities in the application layer. Network-level traffic filtering is powerless to stop such attacks.

Encrypted and Authenticated Connectivity

As incredible as it sounds, networking protocols are insecure by default! Computer networks didn't build in security, because they originated in the trusted environments of universities and government institutions, where threats did not exist. The foundation of the internet is based on unencrypted protocols, and connections are established based on identifiers that can be easily spoofed. Most of these protocols do not offer security in their basic form—protocols such as TCP (Transmission Control Protocol), UDP (User Datagram Protocol), and HTTP are focused only on packet delivery. Application-specific protocols such as SMTP (Simple Mail Transfer Protocol) added authentication and encryption only as a later bolt-on. The basic networking infrastructure does not utilize cryptographic primitives, transmitting plain-text data over unauthenticated connections by default.

Figure 3-1 shows the typical networking journey of a client trying to view a web page using common networking and connectivity protocols. The process takes place in this order:

1. The client types the domain name in the web browser. The client machine must have an active networking connection.

2. The web browser sends a DNS resolution request to the DNS server. The DNS resolvers listen on port 53 using UDP protocol. Both the UDP and DNS protocol are unencrypted by default. The DNS server responds with the IP address associated with the requested domain name.

3. Upon receiving the IP address of the web server, the browser initiates an HTTP request to that IP address. The HTTP protocol is a stateless and unencrypted protocol by default. Under the hood, the HTTP protocol works over TCP protocol, which is also unencrypted.

4. The website responds with an HTML page, concluding the HTTP response and fulfilling the client's request to browse the web page.

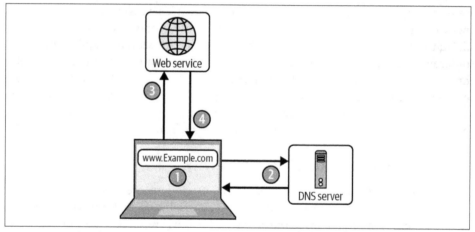

Figure 3-1. What happens when a client requests a web page

In this scenario, both encryption and authentication are missing. This causes a number of problems:

- With no encryption for the DNS request process, an attacker can spoof the DNS response and send the client to a rogue website.

- Because the client is not authenticated, a DNS server must respond to all client requests, which is the basis for a common distributed denial-of-service (DDoS) attack.

- The HTTP connection between the client and the website is not encrypted, which means that an attacker intercepting the network traffic has access to all information exchanged between the client and website.
- The identity of the website is not established, which means that an attacker in the middle can redirect all traffic to a rogue website or inject malicious information.

To solve these problems, we must encrypt all traffic and establish the identities of all parties involved. This is where cryptography meets connectivity. Connectivity and cryptography are two fundamental elements for secure infrastructure access. Without connectivity, there is no way to access remote computing resources securely. Without cryptography, even the most robust identity proofing, authentication, and authorization would be useless.

The interesting thing is that cryptographic protocols are one of the widespread implementations of cryptographic algorithms that require all the major features cryptography has to offer, including symmetric encryption, asymmetric encryption, digital signature, and one-way functions. If a client and server want to exchange messages securely over a computer network, the client and server exchange credentials and keys based on public-key cryptography (asymmetric encryption). To secure the message itself, the client and server use symmetric encryption, because it's faster and more suitable for encrypting bulk messages. To ensure data integrity, the client and server use one-way hash functions that sign the digest of the encrypted message.

The following sections provide details about how different parts of the network stack have been involved in secure connectivity, and how to securely use the untrusted network.

Moving Up in the Networking Stack

The internet we use today was first modeled around the TCP/IP model and TCP/IP protocol suite. The OSI model was later developed to offer more granularity over the TCP/IP layers. But, as shown in Figure 3-2, both the TCP/IP and OSI model serve the same purpose of defining a networking stack, aimed at promoting interoperability between various networking vendors.

When we interact with a web application, the data travels from the application to the network, then down all seven layers of the network, across a physical medium, then back up all seven layers at the receiving end. The lower networking stack and supporting protocols are more focused on getting a data packet from one computer to another via computer network. This means that the further down we go in the networking stack, the dumber these protocols get regarding the notion of users and identity.

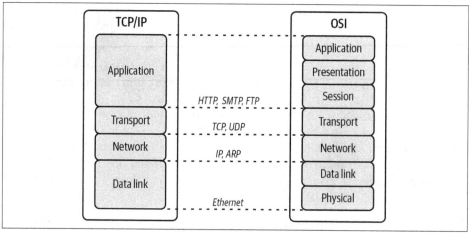

Figure 3-2. TCP/IP and OSI model

Many early attempts to provide network-based security have worked in these lower layers. Encrypted VPN tunnels and firewalls have been long standbys for access control and traffic encryption. But modern attacks target upper layers such as the application layer. Older security tools that work at the lower layers don't understand workload-specific protocols and don't have access to the context required for granular access control.

Moving up in the networking stack makes granular authorization possible because application layer tools have full visibility over requests and responses, including the identities of users. This makes it possible to identify malicious transactions. Similarly, moving up in the networking stack also enables granular encryption. The old encryption tunnels (VPNs) that work in the network layer implemented blanket encryption at the gateway level, leaving all the connections that sit inside the gateway unencrypted. Moving up in the stack makes it possible to encrypt traffic at the workload level, implementing granular encryption for every application. This is why connection encryption based on TLS and SSH protocols are recommended over Level 3 VPNs: these protocols can use the notion of user and machine identity when establishing an encrypted connection.

Perimeterless Networking for North-South Traffic

North-south traffic travels between the user's machine and the server. For example, a client using a web service is north-south.

Traditional perimeter-based access control is similar to defending a physical location: you set up a fence, traffic checkpoints, and ways of monitoring who goes in or out. The idea behind perimeter-based network security is the same: to build an enclosed, safe network that only authorized users can access. When you hide a computer system behind a firewall, it becomes seemingly unreachable from the outside, creating a false sense of security. Many organizations approach secure access by relying on a network perimeter guarded by a firewall.

One problem with a perimeter-based security approach is that the perimeter has become complicated and fuzzy. The environment today includes services and endpoints offered and managed by a growing crowd of public providers, myriad devices that belong to employees, partners, and customers, and wireless IoT devices. Once the attackers are able to get past the perimeter, they can gain access to anything inside.

In the past few years, remote work has transformed from a rarity to a necessity for business continuity. Work-from-home requirements have pushed the security of remote network connections from a corporate-managed branch office perimeter to the public internet, which is out of the control of the enterprise. The same pattern can be seen in the world of IoT workloads where remote access to devices must be possible regardless of their location over the internet. The promise of perimeter-based network security is no longer relevant.

With all this in mind, the future of north-south network security is perimeterless. There can no longer be the concept of an "inside" and an "outside." All network traffic, and the networks themselves, must be untrusted by default. It shouldn't matter whether a client and server are communicating over a network owned by the organization or a public network open to all. Security must instead rest on encryption, grounded in the verified identities of the parties to the communication.

Microsegmentation for East-West Traffic

If there's no perimeter to defend, and no concept of an "inside" and an "outside," then even internal communication is untrusted by default. The access control system must treat every connection, regardless of its origin, the same—double-checking identity, device health, and authorization instead of relying on the origin of the request.

This doesn't mean that the perimeter is completely meaningless! Network security still has its place in Zero Trust but needs to adapt to the new cloud and cloud native workflow and operate at a more logical level closer to workloads. This means tracking inbound and outbound connections, firewalling networks inside cloud clusters, and creating logical boundaries based on network clusters. In cloud native terminology, these techniques are known as *workload isolation* and *microsegmentation*, isolating workloads into the smallest possible cluster of network and computing resources so that the compromise of one cluster does not lead to the easy compromise of another cluster. Microsegmentation used to be all but impossible in the old data center and virtualization software deployment era, because of high manual overhead and the likelihood of having to purchase substantial additional hardware.

Thanks to the cloud and cloud native environments, and their wide implementation of virtual networking, it is relatively easy to isolate workloads to separate network segments so that the compromise of one application and services cannot pivot to another network segment by default.

Microsegmentation also gives us the opportunity to manage end-to-end encryption. Encryption keys for both north-south and east-west traffic encryption are unique to each cluster so that compromising one encryption key does not allow adversaries to decrypt entire infrastructure traffic.

Unifying the Infrastructure Connectivity Layer

Modern infrastructure is a mix of the on-premises data center, cloud, and cloud native environments. On top of this landscape, there are many application-specific networking protocols that do not interoperate with each other. This mixture of different protocols and environments makes it very challenging to implement uniform security policies.

Unifying the connectivity layer allows centralization of access across all services and platforms, making it easier to enforce authentication, authorization, and audits. A unifying approach also improves engineering productivity by making it possible to access every service or protocol using a single tool and workflow.

Secure Connectivity and Zero Trust

Cryptography makes secure connectivity possible. Together, cryptography and secure connectivity make it possible to implement Zero Trust. The idea behind the Zero Trust framework is that there is nothing that cannot be compromised. Zero Trust assumes all users, devices, and networks will be compromised at some point, and takes the posture that they therefore can't be trusted. This means moving authentication and authorization from the network perimeters to each computing resource individually.

Zero Trust means authenticating and encrypting every network connection regardless of where it originates from. Zero Trust means there's no difference between LAN and WAN. In a hypothetical scenario, a true Zero Trust environment continues to run securely without any network protection: no firewalls, no NAT, and every server having its own public IP address.

To understand the relationship between Zero Trust and identity-based access, there is no better case other than to learn from Google's BeyondCorp (*https://oreil.ly/Beyond Corp*), one of the first large-scale implementations of Zero Trust security. Beyond-Corp was implemented in the wake of Operation Aurora (*https://oreil.ly/Aurora*), which targeted various high-profile organizations, including Google, exploiting trusted network perimeter security to gain access to systems inside. As a response,

Google redesigned their infrastructure and internal application access with a Zero Trust strategy, authenticating and authorizing every access request based on user and device identity.

Table 3-1 shows how Zero Trust helps defeat both parts of the human error + pivot attack pattern.

Table 3-1. Zero Trust mitigations of the human error + pivot attack pattern

Attack pattern	Mitigation
Attackers exploit human errors to steal credentials.	Move away from secrets for authentication toward true identity.
Attackers establish a foothold and increase blast radius by infiltrating systems on the same network.	Zero Trust: Microsegmentation, encrypted and authenticated connection, and moving access control to the application layer.

An identity-native solution encompasses both secretless identity-based access and Zero Trust security. Achieving secretless access and Zero Trust is not possible without the true context of identity, because identity is the only dependable proof that can be utilized to shift trust away from static, unencrypted, and spoofable factors to those that can be authenticated, authorized, and audited.

## CHAPTER 4

Authentication

From the day that computers became a shared resource, authentication became a necessity. Authentication concerns itself with establishing a user's identity, the important prerequisite for authorization (which is covered in Chapter 5).

In 1961, the MIT Compatible Time-Sharing System (CTSS) required operators to log in with credentials to prevent them from using more resources than their quotas allowed. Although computing environments themselves, mainly located in universities, could be trusted, it became clear that tenants often couldn't be. For over 60 years, computer authentication has been central to the management of resources.

For many years, perimeter authentication used to be the only line of defense against insecure practices, human error, and inappropriate access. Even organizations that were aware of the need for authentication as a perimeter defense didn't bother to add internal authentication to software applications on their own corporate networks. As discussed in Chapter 3, authentication into the "trusted network" used to be thought of as sufficient.

To their credit, most modern organizations today add some form of authentication to internal networks and software applications. The current challenges in authentication are to move away from vulnerable authentication schemes based on secrets, and to address scalability problems while confronting the question of whether a shiny new authentication method supports decade-old database servers and other legacy infrastructure.

The basic task of adding authentication to computing systems has become relatively easy as numerous open source authentication solutions and libraries have come into play. Authentication as a service (AaaS) providers like Auth0 even offer no-code authentication configurations via a web interface.

The challenge of authentication for infrastructure access, however, remains: to pick an authentication strategy that is robust, scalable and, most of all, resistant to human error. The security of even the best password-based authentication scheme is irrelevant if the user writes down their password on a sticky note attached to the desk. A USB device-based authentication system isn't a viable alternative if the organization's security policy forbids inserting USB drives into client machines.

Authentication must treat humans and machines the same. In a complex computing environment, resources can be accessed by engineers, CI/CD automation, custom microservices, and various other forms of machine-to-machine access. The same access control system must be used to enforce policy for different types of subjects. Authentication must be robust, unique, and scalable. Zero Trust means we don't trust the network but use identity instead for access control. Authentication is the bedrock of this approach because it establishes identity.

This chapter discusses authentication factors and a few of the authentication schemes built from them. The typical enterprise relies more and more on multifactor authentication (MFA) to provide hardened security, and single sign-on (SSO) to scale. A combination of SSO and MFA that uses strong factors such as public keys or certificates can be both strong and scalable. In the end, true identity-based authentication, with a trustworthy identity proxy and a second authentication step, moves beyond existing authentication schemes.

The following section begins by examining methods for evaluating and comparing the effectiveness and practicality of three popular authentication factors.

Evaluating Authentication Methods

Three main criteria prove especially useful for measuring the effectiveness of authentication methods: robustness, ubiquity, and scalability. These criteria apply to both authentication factors such as passwords, and the authentication schemes that use these factors as building blocks.

Robustness

Robustness refers to how well an authentication factor resists being broken. The resistance can be further classified into two properties:

- Resistance to brute-force attacks
- Resistance to human error

Brute-force attacks become easier every day. Modern computing processors are powerful enough to crack weak passwords in seconds. As of this writing, a pair of NVIDIA RTX 4090 graphic cards was benchmarked to crack 8-digit passwords (*https://oreil.ly/Tech6*) in under 48 minutes using hashcat.[1] Authentication schemes must be mathematically secure enough to withstand brute-force attacks that use the power of modern computing resources.

Where there are humans, there's human error. We can be easily tricked into giving away credentials. Authentication schemes must help humans commit fewer errors and recover from human error when it occurs. This means making it easier for users to develop good habits and behaviors, rather than encouraging security shortcuts such as writing down passwords or keeping sessions open indefinitely.

Ubiquity

Ubiquity means being present everywhere, applicable to any environment, resource, and use case. A ubiquitous scheme authenticates both parties in a transaction, whether they are humans, machines, or applications. Such a scheme works in any environment, including on-premises, cloud or cloud native, IoT, and both private and public networks. Finally, ubiquitous authentication applies to any use case, including OS authentication, database authentication, web authentication, mobile authentication, and others.

Without ubiquity, fragmented authentication methods for various use cases create authentication silos, downgrading the user experience and leaving weak spots for attackers to exploit.

Scalability

The explosion of cloud computing has brought a galactic expansion of scale. Gone are the days when a text file containing a few password hashes can present even the appearance of sufficiency. Modern authentication schemes must scale unflaggingly in the face of unrelenting demand. There are three types of scalability, from worst to best:

Exponential
Doubling the number of parties more than doubles overhead.

Linear or horizontal
Doubling the number of parties doubles overhead.

Logarithmic
Doubling the number of parties less than doubles overhead.

---

1 See hashcat documentation (*https://hashcat.net/hashcat*).

Exponential scale blows the roof off the graph fairly quickly, making it impractical in even a modest enterprise. As the scale of enterprises and networks breaks new frontiers, it will become increasingly important to achieve logarithmic scalability.

The price for choosing poorly scalable authentication is high operational overhead, which creates incentives for insecure shortcuts such as shared credentials. Shared credentials make auditing and accountability impossible under the best circumstances and dramatically increase the blast radius in the case of a breach or attack. A scalable authentication method is indispensable to make every resource and every client unique and identifiable. A daunting but important antidote to this problem is Zero Trust access, which requires authentication for everything.

We can use the criteria of robustness, uniquity, and scalability as a framework for evaluating existing and novel approaches to authentication. This is important as people make decisions about how to balance the costs of different authentication methods against the risks of insufficient security. The next sections discuss the three most common building blocks of authentication schemes: secrets, public keys, and certificates.

Secret-Based Authentication

Secret-based authentication works by verifying possession of a previously shared credential negotiated between client and server. As we've discussed, secrets are just data—and like any data, they can be copied, lost, stolen, spoofed, or leaked. Nevertheless, passwords and other secrets are the most common tools for authentication. They are very easy to implement, and we've become accustomed to this method of authentication since the early days, in the middle of the 20th century. In the modern age, secrets have taken on other forms that are less obviously passwords. Session tokens, magic links sent by email, browser cookies, API keys, and other secret sequences of characters, at their heart, are all just passwords. It will come as no surprise to the reader that secrets have limited robustness, ubiquity, and scalability.

Secrets: Robustness

By themselves, secrets offer no security at all. Unless a secret is encrypted in transmission, it can't remain a secret for long. It is not an overstatement to say that without encryption, password-based HTTP authentication is absolutely useless. Every password-based system must rely on the encrypted network layer. Meanwhile, it's not unusual for internal applications to be set up on a LAN without TLS, leaving passwords vulnerable to man-in-the-middle (MITM) attacks by anyone who is able to sniff network packets.

Passwords are not very robust, regardless of the method of transmission or management. In an attempt to increase their robustness, secret-based authentication schemes often institute requirements such as password length, special characters, and a brisk password rotation schedule. This paradoxically decreases security by encouraging lazy behavior on the part of the user. When passwords are hard to remember because they're long and full of special characters, users tend to write them down or store them in plain text. When passwords must be rotated frequently, users come up with cheats like adding sequential numbers to the end of a password so they can use it again and again.

A password manager improves things somewhat by automating away the friction that encourages bad behavior. Because they can autogenerate robust passwords (thus alleviating the vulnerability of easily guessable secrets and taking away the responsibility of remembering passwords), password managers encourage good behavior, making it far less likely that users will share passwords between sites or store them in places where they can be stolen. Still, a password manager has to store secrets somewhere, so there is still a vulnerability.

On the server side, secret-based authentication induces another challenge: How do you manage secrets securely? Even with encryption at rest, the attack vector merely shifts to another secret: the encryption key. Even if passwords weren't vulnerable in these ways, the fact that there is no set of standards means that password schemes can be implemented insecurely.

Worse, secrets have a habit of getting around: there's nothing preventing a naive programmer or a DevOps engineer from storing passwords in plain text in code or configuration or logging them as part of an error message into a log file.

When you have no choice, the recommended way of storing passwords on the infrastructure side with any degree of security is to throw them away and store only a hash for each one. *Hashing* means using a one-way function that makes it impossible to recover the original secret. When a user authenticates by submitting a password, a hash of the input can be compared to the stored hash. Using computationally expensive hashing functions and adding random data called *salt* to the hashing process can make it very difficult to discover the passwords themselves. Just the same, companies consider passwords a significant liability even when salted and hashed.

Secrets: Ubiquity

Secret-based authentication is popular because it's easy to implement under any environment and use cases. Passwords authenticate users in web applications, mobile apps, internal networks, emails, and other places. In a nutshell, passwords can be implemented anywhere.

Secret-based authentication is a one-way street: it attempts to authenticate users but doesn't concern itself with helping users authenticate a computing resource they're connecting to. In other words, a user has no way of knowing if the resources they're accessing are what they claim to be. Theoretically, this could be solved by making each user maintain their own list of resource credentials and requiring computing resources to authenticate back. But this creates the famous trust on first use (TOFU) problem: How can you trust a resource when connecting to it for the first time? Secrets alone can't solve this problem.

The one-sided nature of secret-based authentication is what makes phishing attacks possible. If you can't securely authenticate a resource when you access it, you can't know if the resource is what it claims to be. Bad actors have become very good at disguising their spoofed web forms, servers, and other resources as the genuine article. In other words, though secrets appear ubiquitous because they are used everywhere, they really aren't. You can't use secrets to authenticate both parties in a transaction, because they don't solve the TOFU problem.

Secrets: Scalability

Passwords and other secrets impose high overhead, starting with the problem of distribution. For a password to work, it must be shared ahead of time between two trusted parties. With P clients and R resources, there are potentially P x R passwords. Adding a resource requires generating and distributing P passwords. Likewise, adding a client requires generating and distributing R passwords. This means exponential scale to begin with, but that's not all.

To make matters worse, password formats are not portable, because there are no standards for passwords. That means a password generation scheme that works for one resource might not work for others. In other words, it's not just the passwords themselves that introduce overhead, but a growing number of mutually incompatible password generation and management schemes.

Overall, despite their apparent simplicity and convenience, secrets don't evaluate well against any of our three criteria.

Public Key Authentication

Public key authentication is based on asymmetric cryptography and works by verifying the possession of a private key using only cryptography challenges.

Each party has a private key that is never shared with anybody, and a public key that is derived from the private key. To establish trust, a client and a resource exchange each other's public keys. Each party can use its private key to cryptographically verify a message signed with its public key by the other party. This process is safe even over an open, unencrypted network connection, because the private key is never exchanged.

For a quick overview on how public key authentication works, let's review how you use it for accessing servers with the SSH protocol:

1. The client and the server each generate a pair of private and public keys.

2. The public key of the server must be shared with the client; it's stored in the known_hosts file with the public keys of all trusted servers. The client's public key is also stored on the server in the authorized_keys file with other trusted public keys.

3. During connection, the SSH handshake takes place. Among other things, the client and server send each other handshake data signed with their private keys and validated on each side using each party's corresponding public keys.

Unlike secrets-based authentication, public key authentication is performed both ways, establishing trust for both a client and a server, without requiring a secure connection.

Public key authentication: Robustness

Public key authentication stands on the shoulders of giants: mathematically robust asymmetrical cryptography standards and implementations come from a rich history of innovations in cryptographic theory. When properly implemented, public key authentication is practically guaranteed to be secure, because it uses difficult problems that are not feasible to crack with modern computing resources. Public-key solutions include open source implementations such as GNU Privacy Guard (GPG), OpenSSL and others. The standards continue to evolve as new theories and attacks emerge, meaning that simply keeping up with industry practices ensures robustness. As long as we use recommended cipher suites and key sizes (at least 2,048 bits for RSA), we can be sure that our encryption is practically uncrackable with modern computing resources.

Public/private key pairs are immune to many forms of human error. For example, it's not possible to choose a bad, insecure SSH key the way you can with a password. A properly configured public key authentication system will not accept keys that do not adhere to a specific standard that specifies the cipher algorithm and a bit length. The public key is public, so it doesn't matter who knows it; the private key is a secret, making it subject to theft, sharing, copying, and other vulnerabilities common to other kinds of secrets—but at least it's not likely to be copy-pasted into an email, or written on a sticky note on anyone's desk, so the private key is still somewhat better than a password.

Public key authentication: Ubiquity

Public key authentication relies on every party (subject and object) having its own key pair, enabling each to authenticate the other. For example, in SSH, servers can authenticate users, but users can authenticate servers too. Although public key authentication is not as simple as password-based authentication, it can be used to authenticate anything as long as the underlying client implementation supports key generation and storage.

Public key authentication: Scalability

Public key authentication offers more security when compared with passwords and all forms of secret-based authentication. Public keys are also more scalable than passwords because they can be distributed in the open. Public keys are also insensitive to sharing or even loss: they are designed to be shared and regenerated.

But public key authentication still suffers from exponential scalability problems. Recall the SSH public key maintenance problem from "Certificates as Public Keys" on page 43. When an engineer joins a company, their public key must be uploaded to all the SSH servers in the scope of access. When that engineer leaves the company, their public key must be purged from the list of trusted keys on all servers. Similarly, when a new server comes online, its public key must be shared with everyone who needs secure access. This creates a lot of overhead. Every engineer keeps a list of public keys for all servers, and every machine needs to have a list of all engineers' public keys. This means that public key authentication, while robust and ubiquitous, fails on scalability.

Certificate-Based Authentication

Certificate-based authentication is based on public key authentication, with one additional attribute: all public keys must be digitally signed by the CA. A certificate is a public key supplemented with metadata and digitally signed. Besides the digital signature, certificates also have built-in expiration dates and offer the ability to attach metadata that can express nuanced authorizations.

Certificates: Robustness

Certificates offer the same robustness as public-private key pairs, with additional protections. Every certificate has an expiration date that makes it obsolete and useless after a set period of time. Even if an attacker has the formidable computing resources to try cracking a certificate's encryption with brute force, the expiration date limits the time available for the attack. Certificates are also revocable. If a certificate (or its owner) is compromised, it can be rendered inert. A certificate's metadata can pin a certificate to the context of its usage, making it valid only when used from a specific IP address, for example. The metadata can also contain specific, often temporary authorizations, reducing the blast radius of damage in the event that all other protections fail.

The most robust security feature that certificate-based authentication brings to the table is the ability to attest to an identity. Public key authentication works very well, but it still fails to establish trust: How can you ensure that a client or server is who it claims to be? For example, let's take the example of a known_hosts file for SSH. This file provides trustworthy identification of servers in the form of a list of server IP addresses and public keys in the following format:

```
192.168.1.12 ssh-ed25519
AAAAC3NzaC1lZDI1NTE5AAAAIOqn+5px2hJsspKZtP7uIlqofFAbDA6WghZjbNPZKdPo
```

We know that it is relatively easy to change IP addresses; if a malicious server responds with an IP address that was previously assigned to a trusted server, the client might just connect the user to this malicious host. Fortunately, SSH is aware of this weakness and warns users when an IP or public key of a previously trusted server has changed.

There is an even better way to solve this issue using solutions like mutual TLS (mTLS). In fact, when certificate authentication is enabled, the SSH protocol relies on its own flavor of mTLS.

mTLS enables two-way authentication similar to public key authentication, but with one additional security measure: certificate verification. The client and server can trust each other based on certificates signed by a CA, rather than trusting spoofable data such as network addresses. Using mTLS, you can provide secure access to server fleets or IoT devices even when these objects are too numerous and elastic to keep an inventory of their network addresses. The broader TLS mechanism helps prevent phishing, brute force, credential stuffing, spoofing, and MITM attacks, and makes sure that API requests come from legitimate, authenticated users.

The mTLS communication works like this:

1. The client connects to the server.
2. The server presents its certificate signed by a mutually trusted CA.
3. The client verifies the server's certificate using the CA's public key and responds with its own certificate.
4. The server verifies the client's certificate using the CA's public key and grants access.

From this point on, the client and server exchange information over an encrypted connection.

Certificates are resilient against human error. They are difficult to misuse in the first place, because much of the work such as certificate generation, verification, rotation, and revocation is automated away by the standardized protocols that use them. In the event a private key is lost, shared, stolen, or otherwise compromised, the expiration date prevents the certificate from remaining a liability for long. The policies configured by the CA make it possible to centralize and fully automate the process of issuing certificates.

Certificates: Ubiquity

Like public keys, certificates can be used to authenticate both a client and a resource. They can be used on anything, anywhere, as long as the underlying client machine can present certificates during authentication. Fortunately, most computing infrastructure, servers, and services support authentication using certificates. Certificates are also well suited for automation and machine authentication as every step in certificate-based authentication can be automated securely. Further, the digital signature and expiry time help securely assign credentials to ephemeral computing resources, enabling ubiquitous authentication without the risk of long-lived credentials.

Certificates are highly portable and easy to automate because they are standardized. There are two main types of certificates in use today: SSH certificates and the X.509 standard. Tools that handle all the manual operation to manage certificate and CA life cycles make certificate-based authentication easier to scale elastically as required.

Certificates: Scalability

Certificates scale logarithmically: adding a client or resource doesn't require additional configuration. Clients and resources don't need to maintain lists of passwords or public keys to remember who is trusted. In a transaction, both parties need only verify both certificates against the CA's public key. With certificate chaining, you can even use certificates to extend trust beyond a single CA, or even outside the organization.

Like asymmetric key pairs, certificates enable both authentication and encryption without relying on an encrypted, trusted environment. This means fewer cross-team dependencies and fewer teams to manage. Because certificates can include any needed metadata, they can express fine-grained permissions and authorizations, along with any other temporary or permanent information about a client or resource.

The highly scalable nature of certificate-based authentication has made them the basis for machine-to-machine trust on the internet. mTLS is the foundation for the secure software update systems used on mobile and desktop operating systems. Nearly every website uses HTTPS (HTTP over TLS, also known as SSL) connections to authenticate into client's browsers.

Certificate-based authentication is the most robust, ubiquitous, and scalable authentication scheme available today. It is one of the pillars of identity-native infrastructure access. Certificates minimize human error, discourage secret sharing, minimize blast radius of a private key loss, and attach a client's identity in the form of a rich metadata to every secure session.

These three factors and others can work together when combined into sophisticated authentication schemes. Multifactor authentication, for example, uses several factors to provide additional security.

Multifactor Authentication

By themselves, all authentication methods are vulnerable to human error. Even certificates, which have many advantages and features, must be issued to users and are vulnerable to phishing at that moment. One way to harden authentication is multifactor authentication (MFA), which means adding additional authentication steps based on independent factors.

The foundation of MFA is that knowledge or possession of one form of credential is not enough; you need several authentication factors: something you know, something you have, and, in case of identity-native access, something uniquely linked to physical you. The point is that no single factor is guaranteed to be secure, but by combining factors you can achieve very high levels of security.

Although implementing MFA enhances security significantly, some MFA solutions are less secure than others and may allow bad actors to bypass or defeat them. For example, SMS-based MFA is considered vulnerable as techniques such as SIM (subscriber identity module) swapping can allow access to OTP (one-time password) codes from a hijacked phone number. Yet SMS-based MFA is still more secure than single-factor authentication.

One method of MFA is generating OTPs using a hash-based message authentication code (HMAC), a technique that uses a hash function to symmetrically generate the OTP. A seed value is preshared between client and server, which when fitted to a HMAC function will create identical codes on both the client and server, without the need to transmit the codes over the network. HMAC-based OTPs (HOTPs) use a counter that updates on each authentication request. The HOTP remains valid until the next request. The counter is known as a "moving factor" because it changes from one authentication request to another.

Another OTP method uses a time-based one-time password (TOTP), a type of HOTP that uses time as the moving factor. Each TOTP remains valid for a duration called the *timestep*, which is usually 30 or 60 seconds. Unfortunately, these methods are susceptible to phishing. Although the window of compromise is much shorter in

HMAC and TOTP-based MFA than in simple password-based authentication, users can still be tricked into giving away their OTP codes.

A better way to implement MFA is based on biometric factors. Biometric factors attempt to capture the "something you are" component of MFA by encoding aspects of your physical self—your face, fingerprint, or retina, for example. Biometric factors also provide proof of presence, asserting that the authenticating principle is physically present and that the credentials are not stolen and reused.

Single Sign-On

Single sign-on (SSO) allows users to authenticate once, then access various resources without further authentication. There are two main benefits of SSO:

- Improved user experience, avoiding the painful need for frequent authentication
- Reduced operational overhead, maintaining a single authentication system

SSO providers usually offer identity management and authentication in a unified solution. This makes SSO an easy solution; centralized authentication is convenient when identity is already consolidated. SSO is generally implemented as a database of all users plus the authentication scheme of your choice—hopefully, hardened with MFA. When a user requests access to a protected resource, the resource forwards the request to the SSO provider. Once the provider verifies authentication, the user is forwarded to the resource with a secure session token that provides access.

How SSO Works

The core idea of SSO is to authenticate users once and allow them to log in anywhere. There are three primary SSO methods: domain credentials, credential injection, and federated authentication.

SSO with domain credentials

One approach to SSO uses Lightweight Directory Access Protocol (LDAP), an open standard for accessing directories securely over a network, or the Microsoft Active Directory (AD) service, a directory service developed by Microsoft for Windows domain networks that is directed toward similar goals. In this scheme, the user has a single set of credentials to authenticate with servers and networks on the same domain. When the user makes a request, the application forwards the credentials to the LDAP or AD server for validation.

SSO with credential injection

Some implementations rely on credential injection, in which a user's credentials are injected into a session to the resource as if the user had typed them. There are two main types of credential injection:

- Client-side credential injection, the method used by password managers, uses a browser plug-in to add credentials to username and password fields.
- In-flight credential injection uses a proxy server or bastion host to add credentials directly to the authentication request.

In-flight credential injection is often used in enterprise privileged access management (PAM) systems. It works like this:

1. The IDP (identity provider) stores all credentials, including passwords, API tokens, and private keys.
2. When a client makes a request, the request is routed through a proxy server or bastion host.
3. The proxy server or bastion host retrieves credentials from the IDP's secure credential vault, injects them into the request, and forwards the request to the application or server.

An advantage of in-flight credential injection is that the access control system can enforce credential life cycle management in the background and the credentials need not be shared with developers and engineers. But credential injection is a solution to a problem created by secrets in the first place. Where there are secrets, there is always a risk of them getting stolen.

SSO with federated authentication

What SSO does for a single domain, federated authentication does across multiple domains. An identity provider usually implements both SSO and federated authentication in a single solution, to provide a single sign-on experience within and across domains in the enterprise. Federated authentication stitches together identity management systems running on multiple domains to allow users to access resources with a single set of credentials. Identity providers have converged on standards such as SAML (*https://oreil.ly/saml*) and OpenID Connect (*https://oreil.ly/openid*) to enable authentication flows between different IDPs and federated authentication providers built by different companies. This makes federated authentication a keystone in retaining true representation of identity throughout the authentication process.

By dramatically reducing the operational overhead of authentication, SSO makes it easier to implement the Zero Trust access principles of authenticating all resources, and helps organizations move away from protecting only the perimeter.

Beyond Traditional SSO

While SSO helps solve authentication scaling problems, it is not without flaws. The fear of SSO becoming a single point of failure is not uncommon, and popular SSO providers have themselves fallen victim to infrastructure attacks. For this reason, some organizations employ a tiered SSO approach, where particularly security sensitive resources are protected by more than one SSO system.

The other problem with traditional SSO solutions is that they mostly focus only on HTTP protocol and web applications. A typical computing infrastructure uses numerous other protocols such as RDP, SSH, and numerous database protocols. Most traditional SSO solutions don't support SSO authentication to these protocols, and thereby create bad user experience and operational overhead. Conversely, infrastructure-specific access platforms solve this problem by offering SSO for all common protocols in a modern cloud native infrastructure stack, tying together authentication-based practices.

Finally, most existing SSO systems aren't *identity native* because they proxy the identity of a user with a token or cookie—a secret—that doesn't carry identifying information with it. To implement identity-native authentication requires a signed certificate bound to the identity of a user or a machine.

Identity-Native Authentication

An identity-native authentication access system moves beyond secret-based traditional SSO, providing a proxy that faithfully represents identity in the digital realm. It unifies authentication for humans and machines across all common infrastructure protocols and uses certificates as a mechanism for carrying user and device identity. This effectively leads to a second layer of authentication. First, the user (or machine) presents credentials—ideally, multifactor—to obtain a signed certificate that proves identity for the session. That certificate then becomes the credential for resource access, likely in an SSO scheme.

An identity-native authentication system proposes a different authentication workflow than using a traditional SSO workflow. In an identity-native authentication system, instead of managing credentials centrally in an IdM database, users are supplied with web authentication (WebAuthn) compatible devices, procured by the organization where device certificates are signed by trusted CA.

SSO authentication then involves credentials that are managed entirely at the user's end. This makes the SSO portal just a credential exchange and computation portal rather than a perimeter gateway. The following sections discuss a few important topics in the establishment, authentication, and preservation of digital identity.

Identity Proofing

In Chapter 2, we asserted that identity proofing was the foundation of an identity-native system (see "Identity and Access Management" on page 17). Identity proofing and authentication seem similar at first glance: both are used to verify identity. But there's a difference between the two, especially in the context of identity-native access control.

Remember: an *identity* is a collection of physical attributes, and a *credential* is just data associated with an identity for verification purposes. Identity proofing, then, is the process of verifying and attesting physical attributes to grant a credential for a user to present during authentication. An authentication system uses sets of challenges to prove possession of credentials, verifying that each credential is signed by a trusted CA before granting access to protected resources.

Figure 4-1 shows how identity proofing and authentication work together. There are five steps involved:

1. The user has a set of credentials, such as driver license and birth certificate, to prove real-world identity.

2. Identity proofing verifies these credentials, usually as a part of a new employee onboarding. The same mechanism is applied to a device issued to an employee, registering its real-world credentials (TPM) with the access control system.

3. Once the user and device identities are established, the user can request a new credential (certificate) that is issued by a common trusted certificate authority (CA) that is a part of the access control system.

4. The user presents this credential to gain access to desired resources.

5. Before granting access, the authentication system uses various authentication challenges to verify possession of the credential and verifies that the credential is signed by a trusted CA.

Steps 2 and 3 involve a process called *device attestation*, discussed in the next section.

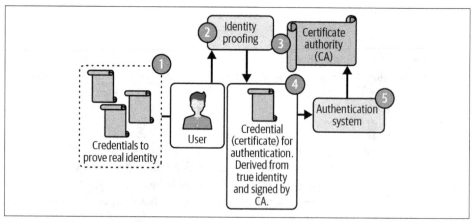

Figure 4-1. The steps in identity proofing and authentication

Device Attestation

Device attestation, also called *device trust*, means ensuring that the computers and other devices humans use to remotely access information are trusted. Only trustworthy devices are allowed to remotely access infrastructure. A modern implementation of device trust takes advantage of TPMs that are present on many modern laptops and virtually all smartphones. A TPM is like biometrics for computers because it gives each device a unique identity backed by hardware. Device attestation establishes trust as follows:

1. A device is enrolled into the access control system used by the organization. This creates an identity record for the device.

2. The device identity is associated with the identity of a person who owns or controls it.

3. Authentication uses the combination of these two identities (human and machine) to establish trust and issue a certificate that allows specific infrastructure access for a specified period of time.

Linking both identities to the physical attributes of a device (TPM) and a human (fingerprint) removes all secrets and eliminates human error from the authentication process.

On one hand, device attestation can be considered an advanced form of MFA. Because a laptop is something you own, it becomes just an authentication factor. A broader and more profound implication of device attestation is that authentication must be performed not only for humans, but also for machines. Device attestation is recommended on the server side too: servers must enroll into the access control system and be given unique identities to become trustworthy.

Device attestation offers additional benefits directly related to secure access. For example, it can ensure that only devices with up-to-date software are allowed to access infrastructure. Another important use of device attestation is as an authenticator for WebAuthn.

WebAuthn

WebAuthn (*https://oreil.ly/webauthn*) is a project intended to standardize authentication with public-key cryptography and MFA. Typically, the user uses a TPM-supported device as authenticator. A private key is derived from a biometric factor, such as by using Touch ID, Face ID, etc. Then the user enrolls the WebAuthn device to the server. Only public keys are uploaded in this case. After enrollment, the device stores an asymmetric key pair. Authentication uses a signature generated from the private key.

Authenticating Machines

It is relatively easy to authenticate humans, as we have the cognitive ability to respond to authentication challenges. Machines, on the other hand, must be configured to respond to authentication challenges automatically. This requirement, often paired with static credentials (secrets), quickly increases the attack surface. CI/CD solutions in particular represent highly valuable attack targets, as they often operate at root-level privileges for production environments and contain "bags of secrets" to authenticate into everything.

Moving away from static credentials and assigning identity to machines in the form of signed certificates during the time of resource provisioning is one possible way to implement machine authentication. Amazon Web Services (AWS) uses a similar mechanism to issue instance identity documents to virtual machines. AWS digitally signs an identity document for each EC2 (AWS virtual computing server) instance, assigning a unique identity to each server. This identity document can then be used to authenticate AWS compute instances.

Similarly, infrastructure services such as CI/CD communicating over TLS have digitally signed identity data by default in the form of a certificate. Since SSH and HTTP/TLS are the basis for nearly any application protocol offering authentication and encryption, tunneling all connections through an identity-aware authenticating proxy makes it possible to easily implement machine authentication in one place.

The last puzzle piece is to securely and periodically rotate certificates. We can solve this issue by decoupling the authentication client and credential fetching process. An automated solution helps further by dynamically renewing the certificates of machines and services in the background, preventing the vulnerability that would result from assigning long-lasting credentials.

Preserving Identity Postauthentication

Most authentication systems aim to preserve identity in a network session after the authentication process. Commonly, client identity is stored as session data in the form of long URLs or browser cookies. These methods of preserving identity are nothing but secrets, vulnerable to cross-site scripting attacks. Another problem is that session data and cookies are not standardized across different resource types. This illustrates yet another reason why user identity should be stored in a certificate instead. A certificate can safely carry the user's identity "on the wire" in a standardized format that is well understood by all resources. And, unlike other forms of session data, certificates expire automatically, which makes them more resistant to leakage.

Another important factor for preserving identity in a portable state is to use protocols that have built-in support for carrying signed authentication data over the network. Authentication Protocols such as SAML, OpenID Connect, Kerberos (*https://oreil.ly/ kerberos*) support certificates, and attestation, can be utilized to safely preserve and transfer authenticated data across various applications, networks, and systems.

In other words, the popular advice of "not rolling out your own encryption" applies to authentication as well. Use authentication implementations based on open standards such as SAML or OpenID Connect for SSO, which issues X.509 and SSH certificates.

Authentication is only half the battle. Once a user or machine is securely, unambiguously identified, and the identity carried faithfully by proxy into the digital realm, there remains the challenge of proper authorization.

## CHAPTER 5

Authorization

Authorization means giving someone or something permission to access a resource and/or perform a specific action. With even a small number of resources and requests, it quickly becomes necessary to organize authorization into *access policy*, rules and requirements that determine access management—that is, who can access what and under what circumstances. Broadly, access policy is a set of rules that defines how access is permitted.

It sounds like an easy problem to solve: simply create rules based on user roles and resource types, then enforce them! Unfortunately, it's not so simple. Resources, roles, and policy requirements can all change—and do, all the time—but that's not even the worst of it. The primary difficulty of designing infrastructure authorization is scaling it, across infrastructure that is heterogeneous, growing in complexity, and always evolving. As sensitive data travels from one infrastructure resource to another, it encounters a patchwork of access policies that don't always match up. A single misconfigured resource can jeopardize security and compliance requirements across the environment.

Access control policy must be managed by a single source of truth. Just as SSO creates a single source of truth for authentication, the same consolidation must be applied to authorization. In practice this means that all permissions for all computing resources must be stored in one place. It must be possible to provision access automatically. This is a must for securing modern elastic infrastructure. Effective access control must be able to protect any type of infrastructure resource across the entire enterprise, working consistently across environments and platforms. Access control must be scalable and *expressive*—that is, it must be able to translate the security intentions of resource owners into reliable, actionable authorization policies at a granular level. It must be easy to administer and control, providing the centralized ability to create, change, and manage policies quickly and consistently. Finally, it must be transparent for authorized users, so that impediments to legitimate access don't drive them to circumvent security controls.

Infrastructure Protects Data

Although people prefer to think about access policy in terms of data, data itself can't be made secure. You can label data with policy, but data can't protect itself. The best you can do is to enforce policy on the computing infrastructure that stores and operates on data. This distinction is important for two reasons:

- Not all data is equally valuable.
- Access policy for multiple computing systems (resources) must be consistent as data travels through them.

It's crucial to provide fine-grained, consistent policy for every data set, but we can only enforce it indirectly via the infrastructure data set resides on. This underscores the challenge: to design infrastructure authorization mechanisms that can work across complex, ever-changing computing resources running on various infrastructure form factors.

Consider the example of a database table containing sensitive data such as credit card numbers. Protecting this data with consistent authorization policy at scale means that access permissions must be consistent across platforms: the database itself, the Linux machine it's running on, the Kubernetes cluster the server belongs to, the backup destination, and the AWS EC2 API that hosts all these components.

In other words, *access policies must follow data*. This is the challenge of scaling authorization, which this book aims to address.

Types of Authorization

With the rise of computer time-sharing in the 1960s came the need to protect data from unauthorized access. Users needed the ability to share the same computer without sharing their data with other users of the system. This led to the development of access control.

Access control means mediating requests by *subjects*, often users, to access *objects*, using *rights* that determine the kind of access a specific subject is granted to a specific object. The intention is to control every access event within a system, protecting data and resources from unauthorized disclosure or modifications while ensuring access by legitimate users.

In operation, every access request goes through a *reference monitor*, a process that grants or denies the type of access requested. Figure 5-1 shows how a reference monitor manages access requests.

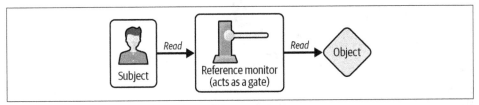

Figure 5-1. Requests going through a reference monitor

All existing access control models have the reference monitor concept in common. To be effective, a reference monitor must be tamperproof and limited to a small part of the system so it can be verified easily, and must provide *complete mediation*, meaning that it checks and evaluates all access requests throughout the system.

The following sections detail a few types of authorization, from very simple to fairly complex, and how some of them work together.

Discretionary Access Control

Discretionary access control (DAC) uses a model of object ownership to determine what kind of access to grant a subject. In discretionary access control, the resource owner has full control over the access rights of their resources. They can grant access to specific individuals or groups and define the level of access each user or group has. Users can pass their privileges on to other users. For example, in the Linux filesystem, you can grant or revoke read, write, and execute privileges for other users or groups on a file you own.

One of the early models of discretionary access control, the *access control matrix*, was proposed by Butler W. Lampson in 1971. An access control matrix specifies the access rights that each subject has for each object. In an access matrix, each row represents a subject and each column represents an object. The cells contain the access modes (rights) that the subject is granted on the object.

DAC (see Figure 5-2) works like this:

1. A user creates a file, thereby becoming its owner.

2. Another user can request access to the file.

3. The file owner can grant access, up to the limit of their own access rights.

4. The second user can grant access to other users, up to the limit of their own access rights.

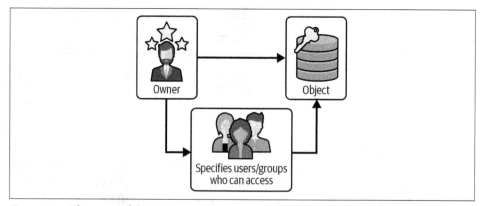

Figure 5-2. The steps of discretionary access control

In practice, there are two ways to implement an access control matrix:

- Access control list (ACL)
- Capability list (C-list)

An ACL stores a column of the access control matrix with the object it represents, enumerating the rights each subject has to access it. ACLs often use groups of subjects for convenience. This is the familiar Unix access control model, where rights granted to groups of users are associated with objects. Table 5-1 shows a simple ACL.

Table 5-1. A simple access control list

	Read	Write	Execute
Alice	✓	✓	—
Bob	—	—	✓

A capability list represents a row from the access control matrix, enumerating the rights the subject has for accessing each object. In this model, rights belong to users, not objects. A capability list can either be stored with the user record or expressed using an unforgeable ticket.

Both ACLs and C-lists are easy to understand, and because they are under the control of users, they can be very responsive; changing an access policy doesn't require going through a central administrator. However, this lack of central oversight can lead to overlapping or conflicting permissions that end up providing too many or too few access rights.

It's hard to define rules based on attributes or context other than usernames in a DAC system, except by associating access rights with credentials. The introspection capabilities of DAC are limited, and DAC is hard to scale.

Both ACLs and C-lists have their own disadvantages. An ACL makes it easy to see, grant, or review rights to an object; but to determine the full list of a subject's access rights requires examining the ACL of every object in the system. To revoke a class of access rights from a subject requires modifying every ACL individually. In a capability matrix, it's easy to see a subject's rights; but determining who has access to a particular object requires examining every subject's C-list. In other words, when a user's role changes, a system that uses ACLs or C-lists requires a lot of work to update the appropriate rights.

Worse, because rights can be assigned by users, DAC makes it possible for a user to escalate their own rights by tricking another user. Suppose a high-level user temporarily grants a lower-level user (or a process owned by that user) higher read permissions. The lower-level user can read and copy data to which they don't normally have access, writing it to an area under their control.

For these reasons, DAC is only suitable for small systems with relaxed security requirements and a small number of users. For situations that require reliable data confidentiality, and for easier administration of policy at scale, access must be controlled centrally. This is the problem that mandatory access control solves.

Mandatory Access Control

Mandatory access control (MAC) takes discretion about security policy out of the hands of the user, managing access rights through a central administrative body. MAC uses a classification system that describes the security level of each object, a clearance label that determines the access level of each user, and a compartment representing a group of people. Access to an object by a subject involves examining the subject's clearance level and the object's security level.

A security level is a pair of values (c, s):

c

The classification; for example, classified, secret, or top secret

s

A category-set or compartment, often used for a department or group

Access to an object is granted only if the subject's security level (c_1, s_1) *dominates* the object's security level (c_2, s_2), meaning that $c_1 \geq c_2$ and s_1 includes s_2 as a subset.

MAC works like this:

1. The administrator sets access policies, defining security levels (classifications and category-sets) for resources and security clearances for users.

2. When a user attempts to access a resource, the operating system uses the user's clearance and the resource's security level to determine whether access is granted.

3. To gain access, the user provides credentials to verify identity.

In MAC, access policy is defined and controlled by system administrators, and enforced by the operating system or security kernel. Nonadministrative users can't alter security attributes for any resources, even those they own. MAC prevents wily users from declassifying or sharing classified data, provides a high degree of data protection with very granular control, and reduces errors by centralizing policy management to a few privileged users. On the other hand, these administrators stay very busy configuring and managing security levels and user clearances and responding to user requests for new access. As users and resources are added to the system, scale becomes a rising cost.

The Bell–LaPadula Model

David E. Bell and Leonard J. LaPadula began working on a multilevel security (MLS) model for computer systems in 1972 under the auspices of the MITRE Corporation. The Bell–LaPadula security model describes security as a state machine that uses both an access control matrix (DAC) and security classifications (MAC) to mediate access to resources. The state machine in the Bell–LaPadula model is defined by a state set B x M x F where:

B

  The set of all possible current accesses

M

  The set of access control matrices

F

  The set of security level assignments

A single state is a triple (b, M, f) where $b \in B$ and $f \in F$.

The basic security theorem of the state machine is that if the initial state of the system is secure, and all state transitions are secure, then every state is secure. This means that instead of checking a system for the result of all possible inputs, it's only necessary to check every possible state transition.

In the Bell–LaPadula model, the classification of a subject or object can't change while it's being referenced—in other words, during a state change. This is known as the *tranquility principle* and helps ensure that subjects gain clearance only as required.

The Bell–LaPadula model defines three security properties:

- Simple Security (SS) Property
- * (Star) Security Property
- Discretionary Security (DS) Property

These properties work together to determine what kind of access rights a subject has to any particular object.

Simple Security (SS) Property

A subject at a given security level may not read an object at a higher security level. For example, a user with only Classified clearance can't read a document marked Top Secret.

* (Star) Security Property

A subject at a given security level may not write to any object at a lower security level but can only write to objects at an equal or higher level. In other words, a user can't copy information from a Top Secret document to a Classified document. This rule tends to move information upward, to higher and higher classifications.

Figure 5-3 shows how writing and reading are allowed in the * (Star) Security Property.

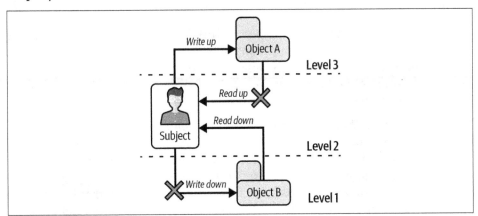

*Figure 5-3. Reading and writing allowed by the * (Star) Security Property*

In some cases, it's necessary for a high-level subject to send messages to a low-level subject. There are two ways this can work: either temporarily downgrade the high-level subject or identify a set of *trusted subjects* allowed to violate the * Property. Trusted subjects are trusted not to perform activities that would degrade the security of the system.

The * Property solves the problem with DAC previously noted. A user or process can't read above its clearance level and can't write below. This prevents a downward flow of information to lower classification levels.

The Discretionary Security (DS) Property

The DS Property is expressed as an access control matrix enumerating the access rights (modes) between named subjects and objects.

In the Bell–LaPadula model, a subject can have any of the following four access modes for an object:

- Execute
- Read
- Append
- Write

Each mode does not imply any of the permissions in the other modes. For example, append mode lets the subject alter the object by adding data at the end, but doesn't include permission to read or execute the object.

Multics

The first and most notable implementation of the Bell–LaPadula security model was in the Multiplexed Information and Computing Service (Multics) operating system. Some of the work that went into the design of Multics can help solve one of today's biggest access control problems: attaching policy to data as it travels through heterogeneous infrastructure.

Multics was a time-sharing operating system in commercial and government use between 1973 and 2000, designed for high reliability, continuous operation, support for a wide variety of applications and environments, and the ability to control selective information sharing. At its commercial release in 1973, Multics implemented DAC using ACLs, along with a mechanism called *protection rings* that further limited access to resources. Meanwhile, the US military had realized that no currently available computing environment offered a reasonable way to handle classified documents. In 1975, US Air Force Major Roger Schell initiated Project Guardian, a research project intended to determine the requirements for military computer systems. The result was the Multics Access Isolation Mechanism (AIM), an implementation of the Bell–LaPadula mandatory access control model. Another interesting aspect of the Multics approach was the way the data storage system made discretionary access control possible.

Files and segments

Multics divides virtual memory into *segments*, each of which is independent, with its own associated attributes and access rights. This makes it possible to share memory between programs and users while enforcing access control policy. Segments are arranged in hierarchies of directories, each of which can contain more segments and directories.

In most operating systems, when a program accesses a file, the system provides only a copy of the file to the program. The file's access rights, name, length, and other attributes are not included, making it impossible to provide meaningful access control to data in memory. In fact, data in the memory could have come from multiple files with different access rights.

In Multics, every file gets its own segment. The process of "opening" a file really means associating a segment with the area on disk where the data resides, then making the segment known to the processes that need access to it. Reads and writes in a segment operate directly on the data stored on disk, and executing code in a segment doesn't require making a separate copy for each user.

The concept of segments solves the problem of *access policy following data*, because the hardware itself enforces the policy. It is this system that makes discretionary access control practical and effective in Multics.

Access control in Multics

Multics uses three different systems to define policies for access to segments: ACLs, a protection ring mechanism, and AIM. All three systems work together, and access is granted only when a request passes all of them.

Multics ACLs. Every segment has an ACL that controls access. Every entry in the ACL specifies a user identity and the operations that can be performed by processes operating under that identity. The user identity can be specified with wildcards to represent groups of users. The operations are different for segments and directories.

For segments, the operations are:

r

Read the file.

w

Write to the file.

e

Execute the file as code.

For directories, the operations are:

s

Read the status of an entry.

m

Modify an entry, changing an ACL for example.

a

Append an entry to the directory.

When a process requests access to a segment, the reference monitor checks the segment's ACL to determine whether the user associated with the process has the proper access rights.

Multics protection ring mechanism.   The protection ring mechanism assigns a hierarchy of privileges to different processes. A lower ring number means higher privileges. The most privileged ring is ring 0, where processes have direct access to the physical hardware. Most applications run in ring 3 or greater, meaning they have several degrees less privilege than the kernel. To provide access across rings, there are *entry points* or *gates* that allow processes to call functions in lower, more privileged rings under certain circumstances. Figure 5-4 shows Multics protection rings.

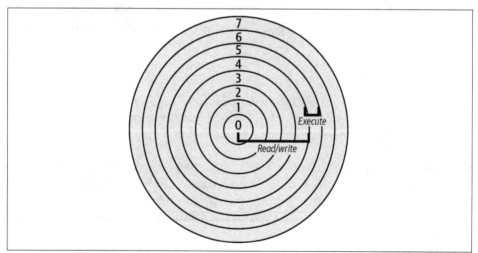

Figure 5-4. Multics rings in a typical user segment

Every segment includes a list of three rings (r1, r2, r3) that define four access brackets to determine which processes can gain access.

The read and write brackets define ranges that determine how a process running in a ring r can access a segment:

- If $r < r1$, the process has read and write access.
- If $r1 \leq r \leq r2$, the process has read access only.
- If $r2 < r$, the process has no access.

The execute and call brackets define ranges that determine how a process running in a ring r can execute a segment:

- If $r < r1$, the process can execute the segment. During execution, the process temporarily transitions to a less privileged ring r' specified by the segment, where $r1 \leq r' \leq r2$. In most cases, $r1 = r2$ anyway.
- If $r1 \leq r \leq r2$, then the process invokes code in its current ring r.
- If $r2 \leq r \leq r3$, the process can execute if authorized by the entry points (gates) specified by the segment, and the process temporarily transitions to a more privileged ring r' specified by the segment.
- If $r3 < r$, the process can't invoke code.

Here's a simplified way to look at the ring brackets:

Write bracket
   0 to r1

Read bracket
   0 to r2

Execute bracket
   r1 to r2

Call bracket
   r2 + 1 to r3

The call bracket lets users call higher privilege operating system programs but prevents the misuse of the elevated privilege.

Together, Multics ACLs and protection rings provide a powerful access control mechanism, but they are still both discretionary policies. Any process with the privileges to a segment's parent directory can modify the segment's ACL and ring brackets. Multics needed a multilevel MAC policy. This is where the Multics implementation of Bell and LaPadula's work comes in.

Access Isolation Mechanism (AIM). The AIM was the first MLS implementation in an operating system. Multics provides 8 information classification levels and a set of up to 18 categories. Every directory stores a mapping from each segment to a classification level and category. Every process has a category and a clearance level.

When a process requests access to a segment, there are four possible results based on the clearance level and category set of the process P (C_p S_p) and the classification level and category set of the resource Q (C_q S_q):

1. P = Q if C_p = C_q and S_p = S_q.
2. P > Q if C_p ≥ C_q and S_p ≥ S_q and P ≠ Q.
3. P < Q if Q > P as determined by rule 2.
4. If none of the above is true, P is isolated from Q.

In Multics deployments with AIM, read and execute permission require clearance greater than or equal to classification, that is P ≥ Q. Write permission requires clearance exactly equal to classification: P = Q. This is a strong version of the * Property (called, oddly enough, the Strong * Property). The Strong * Property states that a subject can only write to its own security level.

Multics security in sum

The three Multics security mechanisms all define access to segments. Each mechanism has its own access definition, but a user's access in practice depends on authorization by all three. When a user requests a segment, AIM checks that the process has the right clearance, the protection ring mechanism determines which bracket the process falls into, and the ACL specifies the permissions the process user has on the segment. The ACLs and protection ring mechanisms are both forms of DAC, but the protection rings are enforced system-wide at the kernel level. The AIM implementation of MLS is a form of mandatory access control. This combination of access control systems is very powerful, but there was more innovation yet to come.

Mandatory Access Control in Linux

Linux is an offshoot of Unix, which in turn was a response to Multics—in fact, the name *Unix* is a pun on the name *Multics*. Unix development started in the mid-1960s, before Multics got serious about security, so security was not a high priority for Unix or its descendant Linux. Out of the box, Unix and Linux rely on DAC in the form of the familiar read, write, and execute modes for groups, owners, and other users.

In 2000, various projects began working on MAC for Linux. Linus Torvalds, the creator of the Linux kernel, authorized the development of Linux Security Modules (LSM) architecture that defined an API for reference monitors. MAC extensions such as SELinux, AppArmor, and others are LSM modules.

Nondiscretionary Access Control

DAC is sufficient for informal access control—that is, environments where everyone trusts everyone else to some degree already. MAC is designed to meet the needs of the military, where absolute secrecy must be enforced based on clearance level. In 1992, David F. Ferraiolo and D. Richard Kuhn of the National Institute of Standards and Technology (NIST) argued for something in between DAC and MAC: a nondiscretionary access control (NDAC) system called role-based access control (RBAC). RBAC is one of the most prevalent forms of NDAC, but there are others. The following sections describe the advantages and disadvantages of several NDAC models.

Role-based access control

RBAC creates an abstraction layer between the subject and object, introducing the idea of a *role* that performs certain types of tasks and therefore needs specific kinds of access to particular resources. An individual user can have one or many roles, and many users can have the same role at the same time.

Often, the roles defined for access control are analogous to real roles in an organization. Programmers, managers, and the company's human resources department all have different access needs. In this model, a programmer's role has access to the appropriate parts of the source control repository, but no access to employee records.

The RBAC model is very effective at scale. When someone leaves a company or moves to a different permission, it's easy to set the new permissions by removing or adding roles from the user's profile. On the other hand, it's hard to express exceptions on a per-user basis; RBAC isn't fine-grained enough to handle every access control use case. Furthermore, it isn't always easy to change role definitions, partly because that act requires examining the ramifications of changing permissions for hundreds or thousands of users in one fell swoop.

Attribute-based access control

Attribute-based access control (ABAC) is a finer-grained alternative to RBAC. While RBAC groups permissions into roles, ABAC determines access based on the attributes of the user, environment, or resource—or all three:

- User attributes include the role but can also mean things like the user's ID or name, security clearance, or position in the organizational hierarchy.
- Environment attributes can include the resource location, access time, and other factors such as the current threat alert level in the organization.
- Resource attributes can include the owner, creation date, and factors such as classification or file name.

ABAC provides a great deal of flexibility in the factors evaluated to determine access. A common use case is to limit role-based access to certain times or locations. For example, a bank might only allow tellers to access customer account data while the bank is open, or only from terminals located inside the building.

ABAC provides finer-grained control and greater flexibility than RBAC, but these advantages come at a cost. ABAC is more complex and requires both more processing power and more administration time to implement and maintain. Because of ABAC's complexity, it's possible for a mistake or a poorly crafted rule to create loopholes that unintentionally grant extra privileges.

Task-based access control

Task-based access control (TBAC) attaches access control to user actions or tasks. Unlike RBAC and ABAC, which passively apply system-centric rules based on fairly static attributes of subjects and objects, TBAC is the first access control model that takes an active approach: TBAC approaches security by granting privileges to tasks, as opposed to users.

With TBAC, it can be hard to specify granular policies, because even simple task-based access is already complex. TBAC therefore makes it difficult to delegate and revoke authorization. This can be especially problematic in collaborative environments, where the access context is broader than discrete tasks. Finally, the fact that permissions are granted "just in time" introduces the possibility of race conditions, deadlocks, and other access failures.

Privilege Management

Privilege means the ability for a subject to perform certain privileged tasks. For example, the administrator account in Windows and the root account in Linux and Unix are privileged accounts that can perform any tasks in the OS. Compromise of one of these privileged accounts would pose a great threat to the organization or individual that owns the computer in question.

Privilege management concerns itself with the balance between access and security. It's important for every role to have access to everything needed to do their jobs, but equally important to mitigate the ability to misuse privilege, whether accidentally or intentionally—improper authorization vulnerabilities stemming from compromised employee accounts and devices, or from insider threats.

Privilege management works with access control models to securely and holistically manage authorization by crafting roles and permissions on a need-to-know basis, providing timely assignment and periodic revocation. The following sections describe a few privilege management approaches.

Principle of Least Privilege

The principle of least privilege (PoLP) is a fundamental authorization concept specifying that users should be assigned the minimum privilege required to perform necessary tasks. Bad actors who gain access to a user's account can't compromise privileges that haven't been granted. By minimizing the permissions granted to each user, the principle of least privilege reduces the potential impact of such breaches.

To implement the principle of least privilege, administrators should start with the minimum set of required tasks a user needs to perform, and only assign permissions required to perform those tasks. The conscientious administrator is always asking: Is this the lowest level of privilege for performing this task? Would a lower level of permission suffice?

For example, the AWS policy below specifically allows access to S3 objects under TEST_BUCKET where the environment tag name equals staging:

```
{
    ...
        "Effect":       "Allow",
        "Action":       ["s3:GetObject"],
        "Resource":     "arn:aws:s3:::TEST_BUCKET/*",
        "Condition": {
            "StringEquals": {"s3:ExistingObjectTag/environment": "staging" }
        }
    ...
}
```

This is a scoped permission; it specifies the resources in staging only in the location TEST_BUCKET, and only allows the action GetObject.

An insecure version of this policy might look like this:

```
{
    …
        "Effect":      "Allow",
        "Action":      ["s3:*"],
        "Resource":    "arn:aws:s3:::TEST_BUCKET/*",
    …
}
```

Notice the use of the wildcard ("*"), which allows any action on any S3 objects under TEST_BUCKET.

It's natural to wonder why someone would use such insecure permissions. You can see how much simpler the JSON (JavaScript Object Notation) is in the second example; as expected, convenience once again pits itself against security.

Zero Standing Privilege

The zero standing privilege (ZSP) removes the idea of an always-privileged admin user. Even system administrators don't have unchecked access to infrastructure resources; they are given permissions only when needed. This helps reduce the surface area vulnerable to attack by minimizing the time window during which admin permissions are active.

Just-in-Time Access

Just-in-time (JIT) access is a workflow that supports ZSP. JIT assigns required privileges as needed, on request, bound to a specific time period or task. These requests can be approved using popular chat tools such as Slack or PagerDuty. JIT often incorporates methods such as *privilege elevation and delegation management* (PEDM), which offers tighter host-based control for privilege management, including managed local privilege elevation such as "run as administrator" in Windows OS or "sudo" in Linux and macOS. Host-based PEDM offers more robust security, as authorization can be controlled in the host natively, as a last mile security measure. Another PEDM-like solution involves creating an entirely new least privileged local user account in the OS during time of access, then deleting that user account altogether from the server.

Dual Authorization

Dual authorization is a technique that requires two people to authorize a decision. Like the two-person nuclear missile launch protocol you might have seen at the beginning of the movie *WarGames*, dual authentication is designed to protect the most critical resources, decisions, and information. This helps defend against bad actors within an organization, as well as honest mistakes—human error.

When a user makes an access request, both approvers must authorize the access. One way to do this is using a chat session. While access is required, both approvers must join a session with the requester, monitoring the task as it is performed. If one of the approvers disconnects, the session is terminated and the privileges return to their default state.

Challenges in Authorization

Even with a panoply of modern techniques, authorization still remains complex and hard to get right at scale. The following sections discuss some of the challenges and trade-offs that you must consider as you embark on the authorization journey.

Access Silos

Historically, the authorization capabilities of computing resources deployed in modern cloud environments have grown separately and organically. The challenge that emerges is how to represent any particular access policy across several resources, each with its own island of policy. Different kinds of resources organize access controls differently and can't always express the equivalents of each other's privileges and classifications.

Often, this leads to a costly effort to manually synchronize permissions across different types of computing resources. After all, what is the point of carefully crafting Kubernetes permissions for interns, if all of them can be bypassed by gaining privileged access to SSH or to an AWS API? Unlike authentication, which has enjoyed a degree of standardization through techniques such as SSO and standards like SAML, authorization is difficult to apply consistently across disparate systems.

Meanwhile, it's data that we're concerned about, and as we've already said, data can't protect itself. We can only protect data by enforcing access policy on the infrastructure where it resides, and somehow making access policy follow data across different systems. Access silos make this extremely difficult.

The following example shows why it's difficult to enforce policies that follow data across infrastructure. Let's say your computing environment lives in a public cloud such as AWS. Let's assume you have a database table that stores credit card numbers. Obviously, this is extremely valuable data and it needs to be protected. Let's see how many infrastructure components need to enforce access policy for this data:

1. The database server listens on a network socket and uses its own authorization.

2. The virtual instance running that database supports SSH protocol and follows the authorization policy of Linux.

3. The database runs on Kubernetes, which also has an API. Kubernetes offers its own authorization.

4. The CI/CD solution that performs database schema migrations can also be used to access that data, and the CI/CD solution comes with its own authorization policy.

5. Everything listed in 1–4 is hosted on the AWS platform, and of course the AWS API can be used to access the Amazon EBS volume where this data is stored.

The challenge is to make these systems individually enforce the same access policy. An auditor should be able to find consistent access records by looking at SSH logs, Kubernetes logs, AWS logs, and so on. Similarly, any employee, from intern to administrator, should see the same access rights everywhere.

The problem of access silos isn't just about a sprawl of incompatible authorization schemes. It is more fundamental: the industry hasn't developed a commonly accepted language to describe cloud-scale authorization. Even seemingly simple concepts are defined differently by different infrastructure. A "privileged account" in modern infrastructure can mean anything from an Active Directory domain account to an administrative account in Okta or other SSO solution, to a Linux root user account.

The access silos problem is only growing and is arguable the largest—and most expensive—problem in scaling authorization in the cloud. We need a way to provide consistent, unwavering control over individual resources as they travel from one system to another. As these systems have grown organically and in competition with each other, the challenge is how to represent any particular set of access attributes across systems that organize security and protection concepts differently and might not have the ability to express the equivalents of each other's privileges and classifications.

Privilege Classification

The complexity of technologies used in modern tech stacks makes it hard to think about permissions and privilege, because they can intersect in extremely convoluted ways. For this reason, the notion of "privileged" accounts is falling out of favor. In cloud and cloud native environments that can be fully configured using APIs over HTTPS, a single malformed call can bring a whole infrastructure down. Even a least privileged account can be exploited to escalate privilege under certain misconfiguration circumstances. There are normal looking roles and permissions that can be exploited to gain unauthorized access. And the number of infrastructure resources and software as a service (SaaS) apps will only grow.[1]

---

1 Modern organizations typically use 254 SaaS apps. One research (*https://oreil.ly/KVN3A*) even suggests that in modern organizations, the IT department alone uses 61 SaaS apps on average.

In the good old days, a team would only put effort into protecting the administrative account in the operating system. But the growing footprint of infrastructure resources and capabilities of nonadministrative accounts makes it too risky to apply the old perimeter-based model of "protecting the keys to the kingdom." Nowadays, privileges are sophisticated and complex.

This complexity often leads to "authorization leakage," where loopholes and inconsistencies can be a source of unintended privilege elevations. Even if everything goes perfectly, the differences between systems make it difficult to achieve highly precise and granular policies. Teams end up creating manual exceptions, such as a "special laptop" that must be protected as the only machine allowed to perform certain sensitive operations. Solving the access silo problem requires a single source of truth for policy, which propagates policy to all computing resources that operate on sensitive data.

Authorization for Machines

OS-based authorization was originally optimized for one type of infrastructure access workflow: individual users connecting to a server to perform their work. Today's infrastructure operations are totally different. Servers are virtual, created with code, and their management is fast-paced and automated. As much friction as identity-based authentication and MFA add, granular authorization adds even more.

Every JIT access request disrupts user workflow; worse, consider dual authorization, which pauses the workflow until two administrators respond to a request. Just looking at the cost per minute of an engineer's time, these interruptions can amount to significant overhead. Still, for the sake of security, we humans can adapt to this process.

But human users aren't the only subjects who need access. DevOps practices, by definition, employ machines for automated management of infrastructure. It's counterproductive to break automated workflows with manual authorization processes like access requests. Since most advanced authorization techniques are geared toward assisting humans accessing infrastructure, the bad practice of creating machine access roles (also known as service accounts) with overly permissive roles has grown more popular. This leads to a greater attack surface area for the sake of convenience—sacrificing granularity for the sake of simplicity.

Complexity and Granularity

Creating a granular policy means crafting roles with the smallest sets of privileges required to complete their tasks. This is not a simple task, because these granular permissions quickly explode in numbers, generating massive complexity.

Consider the challenge of authoring an AWS IAM policy for EC2. At the time of writing this book, there are five top-level actions: list, read, tagging, write, and permissions management. If we further drill down into these actions, the list action has 162 subactions, the read action has 29 subactions, the tagging action has 2 subactions, the write action has 387 subactions, and the permission management action has 5 subactions. That's a total of 585 actions that can be used to create granular policy for an EC2 service. For reference, AWS has over 200 cloud services. And this is only one example covering the built-in services offered by AWS. If you host a custom database inside an EC2 instance, you also need to account for authorizing database users. On a hybrid infrastructure with multiple point solutions and cloud service providers, you quickly arrive at a gigantic number of possible policy combinations that can be created using the principle of least privilege.

When crafting policies, there are only two options for administrators: either spend countless engineering hours crafting a perfect policy, or grant root privilege with a wildcard assignment. While root and wildcard assignment are over-privileged permissions that pose security risks, crafting perfect policy isn't an easy task either. It involves numerous trials and errors and multiple back-and-forth communications with engineers to define a "perfect" policy that gets the job done. It's very difficult to strike a good balance between security, compliance, and engineering productivity.

It doesn't end there! Role sharing, role assuming, and impersonation are common practices to reduce the number of new roles; but these techniques also create opportunities for role exploits.

Consider the scenario shown in Figure 5-5.

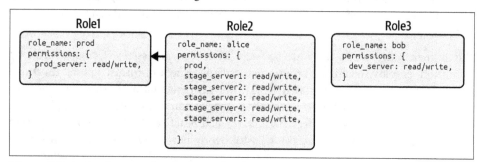

Figure 5-5. A simple example of roles in development, staging, and production

There are three roles defined:

1. `prod` can access `prod_server`.

2. `alice` inherits the `prod` role and can also access `stage_server`.

3. `bob` can access `dev_server`.

One day, Bob needs one-time access to multiple staging servers. Since it's a one-time access, the administrator wants to avoid the hassle of updating the bob role with all the details of staging servers and decides to allow Bob to assume the `alice` role just this once. Figure 5-6 shows what this looks like.

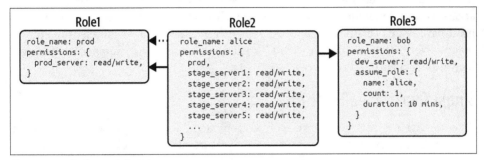

Figure 5-6. Role escaping

Now, what's stopping Bob from accessing `prod_server`? This is a classic example of *role escaping*, in which one person gains privileges by pretending to be another. This is only one type of *transitive permissions*, which allow unintended movement across resources.

As we examine the challenges of scaling infrastructure authorization, it is evident that there are major technical and operational challenges to implementing secure authorization without affecting engineering workflows, and without wasting organizational time and resources. At the same time, no authorization method can guarantee that roles and permissions won't be compromised. This brings us to the conclusion that traditional authorization methods, based on statically defined policies, don't scale to meet the needs of complex cloud environments.

There are, however, some practices that help.

Identity and Zero Trust

In the context of identity native infrastructure access, it's important to reduce the dependence on static privilege management, which has been shown to be ineffective. Secure authorization systems must acknowledge that policies and permissions can be compromised at some point and must implement measures to minimize the impact of an attack. This means taking a step back and looking at authorization through the lenses of identity and Zero Trust. Here are a few ways to take that approach.

Identity First

First and foremost, access policy must allow only proven identities, with no exceptions. Shared accounts are vulnerable to role escaping, which negates the benefits of access control. In an identity-first system, all clients (subjects) and resources (objects) must have issued certificates supplied with rich metadata that is sufficient to enforce policy. Even mechanisms like RBAC are effective only when applied to the true identities of clients and resources.

Single Source of Policy Truth

As computer environments have evolved from single machines to large server fleets, it has become ever more important to make sure access policy follows data. This requirement has been realized and implemented via the segment mechanism as far back as Multics. Breaking policy silos comes down to two principles:

Humans and machines must be treated the same way.
　　Using the same authorization system for granting access to attested identities of humans, laptops, and servers removes a major access silo and duplication of concerns.

Centralized access policy must be enforced across different resource types.
　　This means storing access policy in one place and propagating it through all supported resources. This idea is not new, and it has been implemented in open source projects such as Open Policy Agent (OPA) and Teleport. The approach taken by OPA is to rely on resources to implement OPA integrations. Teleport works differently: it natively integrates with computing resources out of the box, with the list of supported resources constantly growing.

A single reference monitor is an essential component of access control. It's important to maintain a single source of truth, in the form of a single authorization engine that works for all subjects and objects across your entire infrastructure. Just as SSO centralizes authentication, authorization must follow the same pattern, moving away from individual resources to a dedicated component.

Context-Driven Access

There is no single perfect access model for every use case. One can debate the best overall model for access control, but the best approach is one we call *context-driven access*—flexibility based on context. Rather than trusting a single role or attribute, it's better to account for many factors: user identity, device identity, device state, and user intent, as well as traditional attributes such as date, time, or client IP address. This makes authorization checks much granular, allowing detection of anomalies that otherwise would not be visible in a single access control model.

Context-driven access is only possible when access is centralized in one place. For example, you may want to grant database access only to engineers who are assigned to database support tickets. But the RBAC mechanism inside a database is unaware of the ticketing system. That is where a single external reference monitor steps in. Figure 5-7 shows a few attributes of a user to consider during authorization in context-driven access.

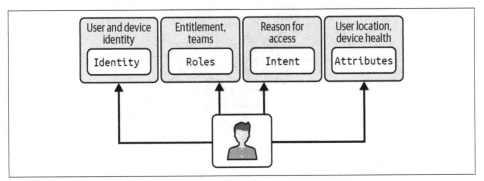

Figure 5-7. User attributes to consider in context-driven authorization

Identity-Aware Proxy

If we consider identity proofing and identity-native authentication the first two steps in identity-native access, Identity-Aware Proxy (IAP) is a core technology that makes a client's true identity available to implement access control in a single place.

All connections between clients and resources go through the IAP, which integrates with an SSO system, a policy engine, and a CA. The IAP's job is to make sure that all clients are authenticated and have valid certificates. If a client attempts to access a resource without a valid certificate, an IAP redirects the client to an SSO system for identity proofing, and then requests a certificate for it from the CA.

An IAP operates on the application layer with full understanding of resource protocols and visibility into access requests. To prevent failure, an IAP must be highly available. To minimize latency, IAP must be deployed as close to a resource or to a client as possible.

In other words, an IAP implements the true Zero Trust model as long as the following conditions are true:

- All computing resources and clients receive a certificate from the same CA.
- Computing resources are accessible only through connections made via an IAP, and only by clients with a valid certificate issued by the CA.
- Access requests are allowed only if the policy engine approves them.

Figure 5-8 shows how an IAP connects users and computing resources.

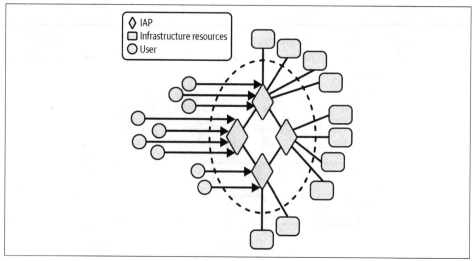

Figure 5-8. IAP in identity-aware access control

Google's BeyondCorp (*https://oreil.ly/4o6oq*) is the first production-level IAP implemented at scale. Teleport was released later, with the intent of offering integrated user experience with IAP, CA, and policy engine all packaged as a single executable.

We'll dive deeper into hands-on examples of configuring such access control systems in Chapter 7, but first we need to address another important aspect of any access control system: auditing.

## CHAPTER 6

Auditing

This chapter includes contributions from
Jack Naglieri and Ken Westin

To gain visibility into what's happening across an environment, it's important to collect and aggregate audit logs from every system, a process known as *auditing*. If a user credential is a key that unlocks the door to the house, an audit log is a record of when the door was unlocked, at what time, by whom, and why. Audit logs can also track which rooms the person goes to and what they do in each room. Maybe they are opening the safe and grabbing some money or a passport. Maybe they can't even get into the next room and are trying to smash down the door! With real-time visibility, we can tell whether the house is empty, or who's inside. This visibility is necessary for an access control system to uphold the strong confidentiality, integrity, and availability that are essential components of data stewardship and compliance. In the physical world, we do this with security staff and entry journals supplemented with cameras; in the digital world, we do it with audit logging technology.

Audit logs, session recordings, and other tools keep an exhaustive chronological record of activity within a computing environment for security, debugging, or system administration. With audit logging, you can investigate effects on a system by examining a timeline of events such as running out of memory or disk space, opening network connections, installing applications, or creating users. Audit logs exist everywhere, from virtual machines to cloud platforms to network devices, and each log is an essential element in tracking the various actions taken in our environments. In security, audit logs are the way teams can forensically understand the extent of an attack or data breach. They provide answers to questions such as:

- Which assets or identities were compromised? (who)
- Which files or resources were accessed? (what)

- What was the timeframe of the attack? (when)
- How did the attack happen? (how)

Audit logs can't always give the *why* behind an attack, but if your access control system supports intent-based access requests, it can provide this information. While an organization moves toward true identity-native access, auditing can help uncover areas of vulnerability, instances of human error, and active exploits.

Logs are useful day to day, not just in response to an attack. As an organization monitors operations, aggregated logs can provide information like:

- What a given identity did during a time interval in the past
- What happened with a particular resource within a time interval in the past
- All current active remote access sessions
- All active access sessions to a particular resource

Logs provide security teams with both situational and operational awareness. Situational awareness concerns itself with the *who, what, when, how* during an incident; operational awareness defines and monitors what it means to be normal. Historically, these questions could only be answered by performing extensive disk and memory forensics. Due to the advances in host, network, and cloud-based telemetry, the timelines of most incidents can be fully traced through audit logs today. This approach is simpler and faster than traditional forensics. The operational side is crucial to testing and refining access control policy, but to some degree logs are always a tool for seeing what happened—usually, the focus is on attacks or breaches, which are, after all, failures in access policy.

Modern log aggregation can help trace the actions of a single identity across multiple resources through infrastructure. In this way, log aggregation helps provide evidence of the way that identity-native access policies are working in practice. One of the most prevalent and important ways of aggregating and analyzing logs across infrastructure is security information and event management (SIEM).

For identity-native access, access to all computing resources and all clients must be governed by a single access control system, which must maintain a real-time inventory of all objects and subjects—the computing resources needing access and client devices used to authenticate. Auditing is key to identity-native access because it makes it possible to maintain a holistic view of the entire infrastructure. Audit must be maintained by the reference monitor and must use a threat detection SIEM system to aggregate, manage, and analyze logs from every service, application, and resource throughout the infrastructure. This chapter discusses the main types of logs, where they're created, and log aggregation with SIEM.

Types of Logs

The two most common and important log types for investigating activity are audit logs and session recordings. Audit logs, issued automatically by hardware, software, and infrastructure, provide a standard set of information about access and other events. Session recordings provide a replayable record of each user's activity during a connection to a host.

Audit Logs

An audit log is a series of rows, each of which represents an action or event. While audit logs come in various shapes and sizes, they typically contain the following fields:

Time
    The time of the event

Resource
    The resource accessed

Action
    The operation made to the system, typically CRUD (create, read, update, or delete)

Identity
    The identity issuing the command

Parameters
    The arguments provided to the command

Result
    The result of the operation

For example, consider the following entry from an Ubuntu system log:

```
2023-01-15T06:36:12.234611+00:00 ip-172-31-29-253 sshd 16901
Invalid user admin from 182.61.42.1 port 59708
```

Here are the fields as they appear in the entry:

```
Time: 2023-01-15T06:36:12.234611+00:00
Resource: ip-172-31-29-253
Action: SSH Login
Identity: admin
Parameters: Port 59708, PID 16901
Result: Invalid
```

The preceding fields provide basic information about the activity. Teams that work with logs need at least this level of detail to gain a comprehensive understanding from the logs they stitch together at the aggregation point.

Notice that in this case the `Identity` field is not very helpful. Anyone can hide behind an *admin* alias. When designing an identity-native audit solution for infrastructure access, you must ensure that your logs contain identities tied to individual users. Logging without a true proxy for identity is toothless. In this case, something like "`alice@example.com`" would have been better.

Every computing resource implements its own logging system. Not only does every different system use a different *schema*—field names and values—but there are many different file formats for logs. The following log formats are most common:

JavaScript Object Notation (JSON)
> A format that represents objects as nested key/value pairs. Most modern services use JSON for logging, which is preferred for aggregation.

Comma-separated values (CSV)
> Nonlabeled rows of values separated by commas, with a row header denoting each column name.

Tab-separated values (TSV)
> Nonlabeled rows of values separated by tabs, with a row defining each column name.

Common log format
> Used by most web servers, a standard format with the following syntax for each row:
>
> ```
> host ident authuser date request status bytes
> ```

Syslog
> A standard for system message logging, used by the Syslog utility, that logs messages from Linux, Unix, and macOS systems (and is supported on Windows by using open source libraries).

While some systems, typically internal applications, generate logs in their own custom formats, this nonstandard approach introduces significant operational overhead and is best avoided. Even when using the standard formats and their associated schemas, logging systems suffer from the same siloing problem as authentication and authorization. Analyzing logs across tools and environments involves reconciling the differences between different systems, which can be a difficult task.

The more consistency you can create, whether at the aggregation point or the logging source, the easier it becomes to link together logs to investigate an identity's activity across parts of the infrastructure. One goal with audit logging is to make it possible to piece together a timeline of all events an identifiable entity has performed within a specific context during a specific period of time.

When you collect access events at a very high scale, it's critical to normalize data types for insertion into cloud data warehouses using ETL (extract, transform, load). Normalization is the process of parsing the original log type and converting it into a consistent columnar format that makes it possible to analyze information from different systems consistently. This process has evolved significantly in the last decade to support the scale of the internet. When considering log centralization and applications to security, you'll need a strategy for making this normalized data come to life.

Session Recordings

Audit logs aren't the only tool in the visibility toolbox. In addition to security-related events, it is useful to record interactive sessions of users accessing resources like the following:

- Terminal sessions established via SSH
- Kubernetes interactive sessions accessing shells within containers
- RDP sessions with Windows hosts
- Virtual network computing (VNC) sessions with Unix-based hosts

These sessions can later be replayed in a YouTube-like interface to investigate a user's activity closely. Session recordings can be small or very large. Terminal session recordings are just an unstructured stream of characters that take up little space and compress well, while RDP and VNC sessions contain graphics and are much more demanding.

Logging at Different Layers

From the platform to the application and everywhere in between, every component should be logging. Generally, logging happens at three main layers:

- Platform
- Network
- Host

The platform layer includes logs that span across the entire infrastructure environment, including native cloud logs and some types of application logs. The network layer logs all traffic between any two entities in the environment. Each host logs its own activity, including application and user events within a single server or system. The higher the layer, the more resources an identity might touch, and the more resources need to be monitored. Figure 6-1 shows the three main logging layers, or tiers.

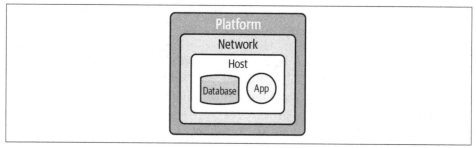

Figure 6-1. Logging tiers

For example, a single environment might contain several platform layers (AWS, GCP [Google Cloud Platform], and on-premises hardware); networks (corporate, production); systems (web servers, database servers, IT systems); and applications running in the cloud or by third-party providers (PagerDuty, Jenkins, etc.).

Different layers use different tools to capture and monitor events. Individual hosts use tools like Syslog. The network uses protocols like NetFlow to capture traffic. At the platform layer, the emphasis is on aggregating logs from hosts, applications, and the network, as well as capturing cloud logs, often with SIEM.

Host Logging

Host logging monitors activity on virtual machines, laptops, or servers. Typically, these systems are the primary point of compromise in an attack because they're directly tied to sensitive resources or have the ability to proxy access to those resources. If an attacker can compromise a machine, they can effectively assume the identity of that resource, causing various types of harm to confidentiality, integrity, and availability.

A typical host-based compromise might be an employee opening a phishing email that installs a malicious application, providing direct access and remote control of their machine. With this access, the attacker can retrieve internal resources, locate new ones, and accomplish their objectives until they are discovered.

Security teams employ various monitoring techniques to observe these behaviors so they can learn to stop similar attacks from the beginning. There are various techniques for securing and monitoring hosts, including both native and third-party logging services. The starting point for host logging is Syslog.

Syslog

In Linux, Syslog is the central logging system. Syslog writes system audit logs as text files in the /var/log/ directory. Each log entry includes a *facility* and a *severity level*. A facility labels the application source of the event (for example: auth, cron, or sudo), while a severity level specifies the log level (info, debug, warn, and so on). Each application creates its log for a specific purpose, such as debugging, privileged command tracking, or tracking local installations.

Syslog runs by default in all Linux machines; modern distributions use an updated form of the original logger, either rsyslog or syslog-ng, depending on preference and distribution. macOS supports Syslog and also has a unified system logger that is similar. Syslog and similar logging tools that run on the host are the dominant source of event logs. Even newer applications rely on Syslog, partly because developers know that these logs are typically aggregated by SIEM. When considering logging policy, aggregating Syslog is the natural first step.

Linux's Syslog configuration files live in the /etc directory and determine which facilities and priorities are routed for local storage or remote centralization. Syslog can send logs to remote destinations using Transmission Control Protocol (TCP) or UDP, or to third-party loggers for more complex routing, load balancing, and protocol support (such as using Logstash to send to ElasticSearch). Configuration files specify the facility matching pattern followed by the destination for each log. For example:

```
# First some standard log files.  Log by facility.
auth,authpriv.*                 /var/log/auth.log
*.*;auth,authpriv.none          -/var/log/syslog
cron.*                          /var/log/cron.log
kern.*                          -/var/log/kern.log
mail.*                          -/var/log/mail.log
# Forward all logs to a TCP listener
*.* @@input.logger.cloud:9551
```

Security-related information generated from Syslog can be found by default in the auth and Syslog files. Table 6-1 shows the information found in each file.

Table 6-1. The auth and Syslog files

Log file	Description
/var/log/auth.log	Remote logins, sudo commands, and privileged cron actions.
/var/log/syslog	Debugging and generic output from all systems. Collecting from here is not recommended because of the size at scale relative to the value provided.

Although Syslog provides a baseline of data for the security monitoring use case, it doesn't give granular context on system state, network activity, and processes running. Several applications have been built to increase granularity for compliance and monitoring purposes.

Advanced system monitoring

In the past decade or so, a variety of open source and commercial solutions have been developed to augment and extend what's provided by Syslog. This includes highly structured and in-depth endpoint telemetry that provides details about processes, files, and other security-relevant information:

- Auditd is a Linux package that provides in-depth system activity monitoring. It works by monitoring each command at the kernel level and logging a detailed context of the attributes of each log entry. Auditd can be installed in most distributions of Linux and is quite popular for augmenting or replacing Syslog, because it captures all commands and provides a great deal of information.

- osquery is an open source project developed at Facebook designed to represent the operating system as a set of Structured Query Language (SQL) tables. Each table can be interactively queried on a system or scheduled for remote delivery. This is a popular option for gathering information such as installed users, applications, open network ports, and much more. osquery can also monitor ephemeral processes and network connections for incident response. By default, osquery runs on a schedule and sends results to /var/log/osquery but can also send remotely to other destinations.

- Several host-based intrusion detection systems (HIDSs) provide additional layers of analysis designed to detect malware and rootkits by comparing local system activity to signatures. One popular open source project today is Open Source HIDS Security (OSSEC), which can be used to complement the tools mentioned above. OSSEC can be configured in a client/server mode for easier management.

Several commercial solutions also specialize in detecting malware or novel zero-day exploits. This category of solutions is called endpoint detection and response (EDR) and is led by CrowdStrike and SentinelOne. They combine the capabilities previously described into a fully managed solution, often with additional services such as threat hunting. EDR works by installing an agent on the system, monitoring proactively for compromises, and logging all process and network data into a cloud service.

Network Monitoring

Network monitoring examines how systems communicate together over various protocols on a network. As we discussed in earlier chapters, protecting the network is not enough—but it is essential in the context of other access control efforts. Network monitoring involves watching the latest log events as they are generated, to detect incidents and other anomalies in real time. Monitoring network data can help people identify malicious behaviors like port scanning, exfiltration, command and control, and denial-of-service attacks. Monitoring often occurs in conjunction with examination of the logs from a specific host. For example, suppose Syslog captures that an admin user started a privileged application (with sudo). Monitoring shows this event quickly. Examination of the network data would then help detect which IP addresses the application communicated with, the duration of each connection, and how much data was transferred.

Network logging provides more context the higher you go on the Open Systems Interconnection (OSI) layers. Layer 4 (Transport) is the lowest layer where logging occurs, and layer 7 (Application) is the highest and richest.

NetFlow, a protocol created by Cisco in 1996, makes it possible to collect information about network traffic, mainly at layer 4. NetFlow provides logs in which each entry is structured as a 5-tuple (`src_ip, dst_ip, src_port, dst_port, protocol`) containing varying degrees of detail depending on the originating switch or router. Most switches and virtual cloud networking appliances contain flow logging as a basic mechanism for tracking communications between systems.

Intrusion detection systems (IDS) and intrusion prevention systems (IPS) use extensions to NetFlow to track layer 7 data, including in-depth protocol information, request/response information, certificate data, and more. There are numerous open source and commercial network monitoring systems with different capabilities, designed to provide visibility to help detect and stop network intrusions.

Log Aggregation

A single log provides only a sliver of the whole picture. Each layer comes with separate context, configuration, and methods of collection. Log aggregation helps provide a single source of truth for what's happening (and what has happened) across infrastructure. Log aggregation is the other side of the coin from centralizing access policy, providing visibility into how policy is working in practice. In sum, log aggregation is the effort to break down the silos created by different logging formats and schemas.

This means, of course, collecting and aggregating logs from all three layers (host, network, and platform) and *normalizing* them, or converting the logs and their fields to a single standard representation, so that the different fields from different logs refer to information in the same way.

Together, aggregation and normalization make it possible to:

- Map together activities for a given identity across each layer
- Gain multiple views into a behavior (e.g., network traffic from an application)
- Perform meaningful auditing and compliance

Aggregating logs puts related events from different resources together. For example, an application log showing that a specific user requested a particular resource can be tied to a network log showing that the user's IP address made a connection to the resource server. Normalization makes it possible to analyze these disparate pieces of information together consistently. This analysis is important in investigating incidents and breaches because it helps show a clear picture of what happened. The information can also be part of a toolkit for holistic access policy design, providing validation or testing of policies as they are put in place.

The importance of log aggregation as a defensive tool rises dramatically when the attack surface area covers not just a single host, but a cloud environment made up of hundreds or thousands of virtual hosts, databases, internal dashboards, and other types of computing resources, spanning across several regions and cloud providers. In the cloud, aggregating logs from numerous, heterogeneous resources becomes a crucial and sometimes difficult task. Fortunately, there are several valuable tools available to simplify the process.

When collecting from cloud platforms, it's important to aggregate log information from all layers, remaining conscious of the different resource types and their roles, to ensure the most context is captured. In AWS, for example, the list of logs includes VPC Flow Logs, S3 access logs, CloudTrail, load balancer logs, and more. These services can typically deliver to blob storage or streaming services that can be consumed and aggregated into a single destination for analysis.

Most software as a service (SaaS) applications with APIs have an endpoint dedicated to access logs. These APIs are typically REST-based (representational state transfer–based), providing access to logs within a certain timeframe. SaaS applications can also push logs to cloud blob storage, such as Amazon S3. In the modern IT world, where SaaS sprawls across environments, it's critical to collect logs across any application that might contain sensitive user data to ensure no blind spots exist. One of the most important log aggregation tools is SIEM.

Security Information and Event Management (SIEM)

A SIEM system is a security-focused aggregation system that brings together events across an entire computing footprint and analyzes them according to configurable rules, alerting the security team when something isn't right.

It is important to understand how SIEM cooperates with an access control system. The job of an access control is to enforce policy. If we think of access policy as a computer program, your access control is like the computer that executes it. How do you know the policy is correctly configured? What if your "program" has a bug? Following this analogy, a SIEM is like a unit testing tool. The policy defined within SIEM is a "unit test" that is continuously running, firing alerts when the policy is not correctly enforced by the access control.

For example, let's say an access control only checks for user privileges, but the SIEM has an additional rule: No access outside business hours. One Saturday, a specific user decides to log in to a database. The access control allows the access, but the SIEM flags it as a policy violation. The security team must then decide whether to tighten the access control rule or loosen the SIEM rule.

If all of your access is managed by a single access platform with a built-in SIEM, the aggregation of all access events and the recordings of interactive sessions happen automatically and can be stored in a database of your choice. However, even the best access platform can't support every imaginable resource and application. You might also want to store and aggregate events unrelated to access. It's safest to avoid using computing resources (log sources) that are not supported by your SIEM. That's not always possible; there are times when you need to begin aggregating logs from legacy resources, and this is often an extremely difficult problem to solve.

One of the initial use cases for SIEM wasn't just security for the sake of security, but to comply with industry and government regulations. Without complete visibility into all data in the system, including who is accessing it and how, it's impossible to comply with the increasingly complex data regulations that exist both within most countries and internationally. Here are just a few examples.

The Federal Information Security Modernization Act (FISMA) provides a compliance framework that US federal agencies must implement in their information security plans. The framework outlines security controls to protect sensitive data. These controls also apply to service providers and third-party vendors doing work with the government. The Federal Risk and Authorization Management Program (FedRAMP) is a standardized approach to authorization, security assessment, and monitoring for cloud services. Cloud service providers who want to offer their services to the US government must complete an independent security assessment conducted by a qualified third party to ensure compliance with FISMA.

Payment Card Industry Data Security Standard (PCI DSS) is a compliance framework for the payment card industry that deals with how credit card data is handled. There are 12 different requirements defining how data is stored, transmitted, and secured. Key data sources required to meet this mandate include firewalls, antivirus, and vulnerability management.

Health Insurance Portability and Accountability Act (HIPAA) is designed to protect the privacy and confidentiality of medical records and other applicable protected health information (PHI). An organization such as a hospital, pharmacy, or insurance company that transmits or stores healthcare information must comply with HIPAA standards.

Any publicly traded company must comply with Sarbanes–Oxley Act (SOX) requirements. The intention of this framework is to protect investors by establishing more accurate disclosure mechanisms.

SIEM helps organizations meet the criteria for all these regulations by providing visibility into all data, including who is accessing it and how. SIEM helps ensure the integrity, availability, and confidentiality of sensitive data, while also providing proof of compliance in the form of an audit trail.

Log Schemas

As the volume and variety of log formats became challenging to manage with relational database schemas, the role of SIEM evolved. Network architectures became more distributed and applications moved to the cloud, leading SIEM to adopt NoSQL databases, which could more easily ingest data from a variety of schemas. Unlike relational databases, which require the definition of a fixed set of fields from the time they're first designed, NoSQL is flexible. You can add arbitrary fields in NoSQL at any time, as needed.

NoSQL databases such as Splunk, Elastic, and Chronicle rose to prominence for SIEM not only for correlation and compliance but also for data-intensive use cases such as threat hunting and SOAR (security orchestration, automation, and response).

Although not reliant on relational database schemas, the NoSQL model still needed to enforce a single data model (log schema), as log data can have different names for fields with the same value. Field names in logs differ wildly, with every vendor using different naming conventions and formats. For example, the source IP address can be expressed in many different ways by different log sources: `src_ip`, `source_ip`, or `ip_source`, to name a few.

A standard data model ensures that aggregated logs represent the same data from different vendors using the same field. Some of the more popular data models include the Splunk Common Information Model (CIM), the Elastic Common Schema (ECS), and Chronicle's Universal Data Model (UDM). These data models ensure that correlation and searches across disparate data sets refer to the data consistently and reliably.

Storage Trade-Offs and Techniques

Although the NoSQL approach to log ingestion solved several scale and flexibility challenges, this approach also introduced other challenges at scale. To manage data quickly, it was necessary to combine compute and storage on a single node. Log aggregation became increasingly resource intensive, which meant higher hardware or cloud costs. The solution to these problems was to create different buckets for log data:

Hot
> These are the nodes where data is ingested and searchable and are the most resource-intensive nodes. Data is only stored here for a short period, a few days to a week, before rolling over to the warm bucket.

Warm
> As data ages out of the hot bucket, it is rolled over to warm. The warm nodes are less resource intensive, as they are not ingesting new logs. Warm notes still need a lot of RAM to enable fast searching, but do not require as much processing power as hot nodes. Data in the warm bucket is usually stored for 30–90 days, depending on the policies, use cases, and budget established by the organization.

Cold
> Data that the organization still wants to be able to search, but where fast searches are not a requirement, can be moved to cold nodes to save money. The cold bucket is a good storage area for data that is not particularly helpful for use cases such as threat hunting but still needs to be accessible for compliance use cases.

Frozen
> Data that needs to be stored for an extended period such as a year or more goes to the frozen bucket, which is more analogous to a traditional backup. The data is usually not searchable and is kept in low-cost storage.

Figure 6-2 shows the different heat levels for log data.

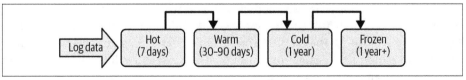

Figure 6-2. Different heat levels for log data

The heat levels represent different cost/performance trade-offs for different use cases. Moving data—from frozen to hot, for example—comes at a cost in terms of time to "thaw" the data plus additional data ingest costs. The configuration and management of these systems also increases in complexity when more data is ingested.

Evolution of the Cloud Data Warehouse

NoSQL-powered SIEMs evolved out of necessity to handle the exponential growth in data generated by security systems and devices. These databases were designed to scale horizontally, making them well suited for storing and processing large amounts of data. However, as the amount of data continued to grow, these databases became increasingly challenging to manage, and their performance began to suffer.

More recently, cloud native data warehouse systems such as Snowflake have emerged as a more modern approach for SIEM and security analytics. These systems are designed to handle large amounts of data and provide more advanced querying and analysis capabilities, which hide the complexities of hot-warm-cold architectures and free security teams to focus on mitigating threats versus managing infrastructure. They also offer better performance and scalability than NoSQL databases, making them well suited for storing and processing large amounts of security data at a lower cost. This makes them ideal for both compliance and threat-hunting use cases. Data warehouse systems are typically more closely integrated with other security tools and systems, such as threat intelligence platforms and incident response tools, further enhancing their effectiveness in the SIEM context.

Log Analysis Techniques

From a security perspective, the primary jobs in SIEM are to detect unusual patterns in your logs and to create a mechanism for responding to and resolving undesirable behaviors. The SIEM must be molded to your threat model to improve the relevance of alerts along with coverage across the organization's defense model. Most organizations today follow MITRE's ATT&CK Matrix to ensure baseline coverage while adding unique alerts specific to the organization's needs.

Cybersecurity teams want to run as efficiently as possible, to resolve breach scenarios, and return their organizations to stability quickly. Security teams have finite time and resources that must be used consciously and with careful intent. Analysis has evolved over the years from rigid systems with built-in signatures, to generalized logging solutions, to ML-based platforms. Teams today should automate as much as they can to enrich alerts, gather organizational context, and validate behaviors from users before attempting manual analysis.

New technologies are helping turn automated detection and response into a reality. Detection-as-code formalizes the definition of threat models and treats them as source code, so they can be managed, tested, and put in production with automated CI/CD toolchains. SOAR ingests alerts and automatically triggers playbooks that orchestrate workflows in response to an incident.

When it comes to log analysis, there are a few techniques teams can use to establish their alerts:

Signature analysis
> Explicitly defining a pattern in the logs by looking for specific values. An example could be looking for any log with a command-line field containing the word `wget`.

Correlative analysis
> Similar to signature analysis but looks at successive behaviors from multiple rules within a sequence or in a window of time. These are best for identifying potentially harmful system processes, odd user behavior, or exfiltration.

User behavioral analysis
> Identify anomalous behavior using machine learning. Certain SIEMs have these models built-in to flag activities that signatures can't see as quickly.

The recommendation is to utilize each of the above techniques to improve fidelity and to help refine access policy.

Log Analysis Example: Modern Ransomware Attack

To understand the role of a SIEM, let's use a threat that many organizations face today: ransomware. Ransomware doesn't just appear on a network; an attacker must take a number of steps to successfully deploy ransomware on a network. Although early versions of ransomware targeted individual systems, today's more lucrative ransomware syndicates target entire networks. The attackers not only attempt to encrypt data on the network, but also exfiltrate the data for additional leverage against the organization, threatening to release sensitive data. The key attack vector in most ransomware cases is the compromise of credentials. After the initial intrusion, the attackers pivot and use escalation of privileges to grab the keys to the kingdom, gaining access to all assets and identities.

We will model a typical ransomware attack sequence using the Lockheed Martin Killchain (*https://oreil.ly/0k9Oa*), which shows the common paths that attackers take to conduct attacks. Figure 6-3 shows the links in the chain.

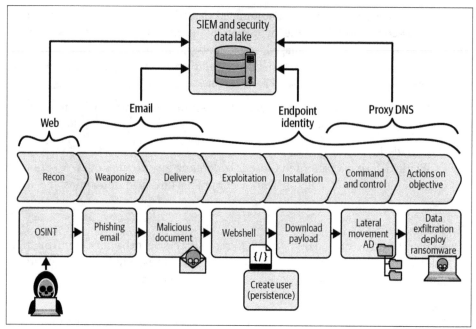

Figure 6-3. The Lockheed-Martin Killchain

As you read the description of the attack pattern, note how the attacker relies on vulnerabilities created directly by secrets and human error.

Reconnaissance

In our attack scenario, the attacker starts by conducting reconnaissance against the organization. Much of this is done without touching the network, but may include scanning, probing, and attempting to access assets using compromised credentials. Although some of the activities might generate alerts from web servers, firewalls, and other internet-facing asset telemetry, the majority of these alerts will be "informational" with low levels of severity, as the goal of the attacker is to remain under the radar. This data will be available in the SIEM, but most often will only be useful in postmortems after a compromise, or to enrich more high-priority alerts with additional context.

Weaponization

In this scenario, the attacker has identified email addresses of key employees who they believe have elevated privileges within the organization. The attacker registers a domain that looks similar to the company's, then sends an email to these key employees with a convincing message and an attached Microsoft Word document containing a malicious macro. The attacker crafts the email to circumvent the cloud email provider's basic email security controls. Email metadata will be sent to the SIEM, but this data usually only includes basic information such as sender, receiver, subject, and possibly some information regarding the attachment—but not its contents. At this stage of the attack the email gateway might issue some alerts but given the high number of alerts from these systems, they are often ignored.

Delivery

Once the attacker is able to bypass basic email protections, the emails with malicious attachments are delivered successfully to the targets. Some of the users may suspect the email is malicious or phishing and may forward it to their security team or report the email as suspicious from within the email system. These alerts may be considered low- or medium-severity alerts. If the alerts are not acted on immediately by security teams, the attacker has more time.

Exploitation

One of the targets believes the email is legitimate and opens the malicious attachment. The document executes a malicious macro and provides a web shell back to the attacker's machine, giving the attacker access to the system. The attacker can now deploy additional payloads and conduct lateral movement. Depending on what endpoint security tools and telemetry are deployed, alerts or events will be generated and sent to the SIEM. An EDR may detect this behavior and isolate the system. If the organization is running a host-level logging tool like Sysmon, then events will be generated and sent, but may or may not generate alerts from the SIEM. In this case, the identity of an administrator user on the system has also been compromised and the attacker can pivot into multiple systems.

Installation

At this point, the attacker uses the web shell running on the compromised system to push additional payloads and tools and can also leverage legitimate tools already available on the compromised system. The attacker creates an additional user on the system and sets up a scheduled task on the system to reconnect to the attacker's machine if the system is rebooted, thereby establishing persistence. If the system has a modern EDR running, much of this activity will be detected. However, the attacker may also implement techniques that bypass EDR protections.

Command and control

Now, with a firm foothold on the system, the attacker conducts additional discovery from within. They can leverage the additional tools now available to them to identify additional systems to compromise, and access key data repositories as well as key systems such as the domain controller, Active Directory, and other services. If they compromise these key assets, they may dump credentials and inventory key data stores, and prepare to exfiltrate data and deploy ransomware to the organization. As the attacker moves around the network, IDS/IPS tools may provide additional telemetry and alerts to their activities, and as they pivot to critical systems, more robust EDR and other protections may trigger alerts as well.

Actions on objective

Once the attacker has gained access to the "crown jewels" and has control over the network, they will conduct their "actions on objective," where data will be exfiltrated and ransomware executed on the network. At this stage alarms may be raised—but it might be too late once the data encryption process has started. At this stage, as the attacker has access to administrator credentials, the attacker can also pivot into additional systems such as cloud environments and SaaS apps.

Attack postmortem

As you can see through this attack scenario, there are a number of points where the attack could be detected and blocked throughout the kill chain. Having visibility into compromised assets and identities requires logs from a number of disparate sources. The higher the fidelity of a given alert, the more context can be provided to the analyst in the SIEM to connect the dots, identify the threat, and mitigate it. The ability to identify multiple stages of an attack is enhanced by the availability of a security data lake where all telemetry is stored—not just alerts. This allows the analyst to have more context for a given threat at the tip of their fingers, rather than having to access several systems remotely, which may not be available during a security incident.

Auditing and Logging in an Identity-Native System

As organizations have shifted to cloud based infrastructure and SaaS applications, the role of identity management has become an increasingly important component of security. Logging, monitoring, aggregation, and normalization work together to provide visibility into how access policy is working in production.

Just as one central challenge of access management is to create policy that can follow data across infrastructure, a core goal of logging is identity-native visibility through aggregation and normalization. The intention is to be able to see what a given user has done, either at a point of time or over a specified period, and how the user's actions have affected every type of resource involved. For an organization on the journey to identity-native access control, auditing is a last line of defense against the ever present human error + pivot attack pattern. Even in a true identity-native environment, auditing provides a form of unit testing, proving that everything is working and giving visibility that helps drive continuous improvements.

In Chapter 7, we'll look at ways to bring everything we've discussed into action.

## CHAPTER 7

Scaling Access: An Example Using Teleport

So far, we've covered the fundamental pillars of infrastructure access: identity, connectivity, authentication, authorization, and audit. By now, the benefits of the identity-native approach are clear. By tying true identity to access and policy to data, you can scale across increasingly complex computing environments without sacrificing agility or security. At the same time, the identity-native approach removes human error vectors such as secrets and perimeter-based defense, making the entire environment more secure and removing the potency of attacks such as phishing. This adds up to the most important benefit of all: making access easy at scale.

In this chapter, we will explore the available open source tools and techniques for implementing identity-native principles to scale access in practice. For the purpose of the discussion, we'll examine Teleport, which at the time of this writing is the only open source project that combines the principles of identity-native access, such as Zero Trust connectivity and secretless architecture.

Access at Scale

Scaling access with the infrastructure needs of a growing organization is important for both security and productivity. As an organization grows, however, the complexity of access increases geometrically across three primary dimensions: hardware, software, and peopleware.

The infrastructure footprint typically grows organically, following the areas where network traffic is increasing. Eventually, this leads to multicloud environments or geographic expansions to multiple regions. Every cloud provider brings its own authentication and authorization scheme, which is different from what's used in on-premises environments.

At the same time, the computing environments themselves become more complex. Specialized databases, Kubernetes, serverless platforms, numerous DevOps tools, an ever-growing number of microservices, and other technology layers increase the height and complexity of a typical tech stack. Each of these software layers has its own connectivity needs and its own authentication, authorization, and audit mechanisms. Every new technology deployed in a cloud environment has its own access overhead.

As the organization matures, engaging with more customers in more countries around the world, the forest of regulations thickens. Every country has its own rules about data and access compliance. Aside from the regulatory pressure, there is market pressure to comply with voluntary data and security standards such as those covered by System and Organization Controls for Service Organizations (SOC and SOC 2) auditing.

Finally, as you might expect, comes the human factor. The successful organization grows, its org chart becomes enormous, and the number of people requiring access to various kinds of resources grows exponentially. External contractors introduce the problems of granting limited, temporary privileges that don't always align with normal roles throughout the organization. The result is a growing need for more roles that express more and more granular permissions.

All this adds up to a need to rethink access strategy holistically. Allowing access policy to grow responsively leads to prohibitive expense, in terms of both cost and time to market. Moreover, scaling secure access under pressure creates perverse incentives for shortcuts such as shared credentials or perimeter-focused security, as discussed earlier.

The solution is to design infrastructure access policy that doesn't add significant operational overhead as the organization continues to scale. The following sections provide guidance for one approach to scalable infrastructure access policy design.

Identity-Native Access Checklist

When designing a scalable infrastructure access solution, it helps to be able to visualize your entire infrastructure footprint as a single giant computer. To gain this kind of visibility, you need both comprehensive auditing and the ability to apply access policy consistently across the entire "machine," treating all objects and subjects exactly the same.

Drawing from the concepts of Multics, this means subjects access objects only via designated access gates controlled by a single reference monitor, which is responsible for both enforcing policy and maintaining the audit log, as illustrated in Figure 7-1.

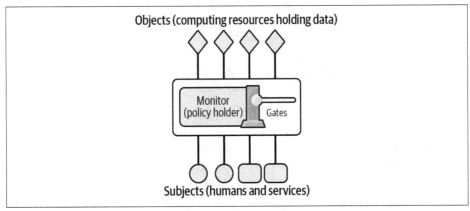

Objects (computing resources holding data)

Monitor
(policy holder)   Gates

Subjects (humans and services)

Figure 7-1. Subjects access objects only via designated access gates

This approach consolidates connectivity, authentication, authorization, and audit to eliminate access silos, which are the primary obstacle for scaling access. In practice, this means focusing on several principles that work together to make identity-native infrastructure access possible. We call this the *identity-native access checklist*:

☐ Maintain a holistic view of the entire infrastructure.

Access to all computing resources and all clients must be governed by a single access control system, which must maintain a real-time inventory of all objects and subjects (i.e., the computing resources needing access and client devices used to authenticate).

☐ Treat humans and machines the same.

In a complex computing environment, data can be accessed by engineers, CI/CD automation, custom microservices, and other forms of machine-to-machine access. The same access control system must be used to enforce policy for different types of subjects.

☐ Move away from static credentials toward identity.

For all subjects, grant access based only on true identity that uses physical attributes of subjects—biometrics for humans, TPM and HSM for machines.

☐ Maintain a single source of truth for policy.

Just as single sign-on (SSO) created a single source of truth for authentication, the same idea must be applied to authorization. In practice this means that all permissions for all computing resources must be stored in one place.

☐ Embrace Zero Trust connectivity.

Networks no longer play a role in security in general. Consolidate all connectivity through Identity-Aware Proxies (IAPs) that permit only authenticated and encrypted connections. The number of IAPs needs to match the infrastructure scale, but they must all be controlled by the same access control system (i.e., the reference monitor).

☐ Consolidate audit in one place.

Audit must be maintained by the reference monitor and must use a threat detection SIEM system to aggregate, manage, and analyze logs from every service, application, and resource throughout the infrastructure.

☐ Define access as code.

Automatic access provisioning is a must for securing modern elastic infrastructure. Cloud native access enables flexible attribute-based, just-in-time access policies. More importantly, DevOps-friendly access workflows that integrate into cloud native software delivery enable higher engineering productivity and remove the incentives for engineers to circumvent policy.

The identity-native access checklist is our recipe for scaling access. The foundation is to abandon static credentials and secrets in favor of hardened identity and ephemeral certificates for all infrastructure protocols. In turn, this enables consolidating all four access pillars in one place, making access more cost efficient at scale and far easier to use.

Necessary Components

Building an identity-native access control system involves a number of technologies that work together. For starters, we need:

- Identity management (IdM) platform
- Infrastructure access platform that maintains an inventory of all resources and devices, issues certificates, and enforces Zero Trust connectivity via identity-aware proxies
- Security information and event management (SIEM)

To avoid unnecessary dependency on proprietary technologies for core capabilities, we recommend building an access control system with open source components and using open standards wherever possible.

For the IdM, you can use a SaaS platform such as Okta or Active Directory. For smaller teams, even GitHub SSO can suffice. Our requirements for an IdM are:

- To be a single source of truth for all users within an organization and their roles
- To provide phishing-proof authentication
- To support open standards for authentication, such as SAML or OpenID Connect

To provide a holistic view of all trusted resources, we need a centralized and automatically updating database of the following:

- Trusted people
- Trusted client devices, such as laptops with Touch ID and other forms of TPM
- Other forms of trusted hardware biometric devices, such as Yubikeys
- Trusted devices such as servers, VMs, or cloud instances
- Trusted computing resources: databases, Kubernetes clusters, and internal web applications such as CI/CD systems or monitoring dashboards

The IdM provides a database of trusted employees and their roles, but it does not keep track of devices, nor does it have a way to define universal access policy. To solve this problem, we integrate the IdM and infrastructure access platform.

The infrastructure access platform maintains its own database of all trusted devices and computing resources and combines this information with identities stored by the IdM. This effectively consolidates policy definition and enforcement in one place. The infrastructure access platform also includes an identity-aware proxy, which governs all connections and sessions happening across the environment to ensure that the same policy is enforced everywhere. This creates a single collection point for all security events so they can be aggregated and exported into the SIEM or a threat detection tool.

In the precloud era, privileged access management (PAM) systems were the standard for access control to critical infrastructure, but legacy PAM solutions are ill-suited to modern cloud environments. They focus on managing static credentials, do not natively support cloud workloads like Kubernetes or services like Amazon RDS, and do not fit into the DevOps cycle, which requires defining infrastructure itself and its access policy as code.

In this chapter, the infrastructure access platform we will use to illustrate these concepts is Teleport, an open source solution hosted on GitHub (*https://oreil.ly/teleport*) and available as a commercial self-hosted and SaaS product.

There are many SIEM solutions such as Splunk, Sumo Logic, and Panther. The SIEM automatically aggregates and stores logs, events, and session recordings so they're available for analysis. In effect, the SIEM acts as a testing and validation tool for the policy defined and maintained by the other components of the access system.

The Teleport Infrastructure Access Platform

Teleport is a dependency-free binary executable that runs on the infrastructure side to provide secure access over SSH and other protocols. The following sections describe the basic architecture of Teleport.

The Cluster

The main part of the architecture is the *cluster*, which expresses a scope of trust enforcement.

A cluster always contains a certificate authority (CA) at its core, which issues SSH and X.509 certificates for humans, machines, and service accounts. A cluster also maintains the database of trusted resources, which makes it easy to create resource groups and isolate them using logical segmentation. The cluster runs the services that manage secure access: the Auth Service, the Proxy Service, and several access services.

Auth Service

The Teleport Auth Service is the heart of the cluster. The Auth Service contains the CA and handles authentication and authorization. The Auth Service stores the user roles, the inventory of resources, and a database of enrolled client devices, and produces an audit log. Every authentication and authorization request that takes place within a cluster is handled by the Auth Service. All other services must be started with the address of the Auth Service to join the cluster.

Proxy Service

The Proxy Service is a lightweight, stateless, identity-aware, multiprotocol access proxy that manages connections to all infrastructure resources. The Proxy Service implements a protocol-level traffic handler, which provides full control and visibility over each access request. This makes it possible to analyze both identity and context of access, which is not possible with TCP-only access proxies. Teleport currently supports SSH, RDP, a variety of SQL and NoSQL databases, Kubernetes API, and HTTPS and TCP protocols. In a Zero Trust configuration with reverse tunnels, the proxy service is exposed on the public internet to allow connections from authenticated parties. You can launch as many proxies as you need, wherever they're needed, to optimize for throughput and latency.

Access services

There are five types of access services:

SSH Service
> For accessing Linux servers or virtual machines via SSH protocol

Kubernetes Service
> For accessing Kubernetes clusters via Kubernetes API

Database Service
> For accessing databases

Desktop Service
> For accessing Windows machines with RDP protocol via a browser

Application Service
> For accessing web applications without public endpoints (behind NAT [network address translation])

You use the access services to enroll infrastructure into a Teleport cluster. The enrollment process is important, because it allows you to establish a *holistic view of everything*: not just all users and their roles, but also all servers, virtual machines, laptops, databases, and everything else.

How Teleport Works

In a Teleport cluster, humans and machines (service accounts) are treated the same. They can only access infrastructure resources through an identity-aware, multiprotocol proxy, which ensures that only authenticated and encrypted connections are allowed. The higher up in the OSI model these connections are, the more context is available to enable both connectivity and authorization (i.e., policy enforcement). Figure 7-2 shows how the Teleport components work together.

All access from subjects to objects is mediated by the identity-aware proxy, which plays the role of the reference monitor. The identity-aware proxy communicates with the rest of the IA platform via an API.

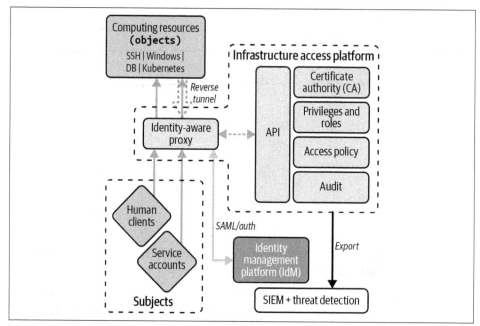

Figure 7-2. How the Teleport access control system works

Before Teleport allows a session to connect, the proxy checks whether the client can supply a valid certificate. Teleport supports two certificate types: SSH and X.509. In practice, these cover all commonly used infrastructure protocols. If a client is not authenticated yet, Teleport redirects it to the IdM via SAML for authentication. Service accounts can authenticate and receive a certificate via an API.

To become trusted and accessible, computing resources must be enrolled into the cluster. This prevents impersonation attacks and resolves the trust on first use (TOFU) problem. The CA keeps track of the identities of all resources, issuing self-expiring certificates for them as needed.

Notice the "reverse tunnel" connection from computing resources into the proxy. You can configure a resource, for example an SSH server, to establish a permanent outbound encrypted connection to the proxy. This enables true Zero Trust networking. The server doesn't even listen on the network, and only accepts incoming connections that are established via the tunnel.

The computing resources and the proxy emit security events that are submitted into the auth service and stored in the audit log. You can export the audit log in to the external SIEM solution. The audit log contains logged security events in JSON format and recorded interactive sessions.

In this model, there are no permanently stored secrets anywhere. Every device, every resource, and every person is authenticated using an ephemeral certificate that is issued based on physical attributes. Employee onboarding and offboarding are fully automatic. When people appear or disappear in the IdM, access is automatically provisioned or deprovisioned. Similarly, as resources come online, they automatically enroll via the proxy, based on assigned roles.

The reverse tunnels allow this model to operate over completely untrusted networks, where each device runs on a public IP address or behind a third-party private LAN. The tunneling works similar to how software updates work on all mobile operating systems: the devices only trust authenticated connections originating from Apple, Microsoft, or Google. With tunnels, devices enrolled into the Teleport infrastructure access platform only trust the authenticated connections originating from the proxy.

Managing Users

Teleport integrates with SSO to provide access to infrastructure. This integration lets Teleport retrieve a user's information and roles when infrastructure access is requested. There are many SSO providers, but for this example we'll use GitHub SSO and integrate it with the Teleport infrastructure access platform.

The gist of the process is:

1. Create an OAuth application in GitHub, using the Teleport proxy for the callback URL.
2. On the Teleport side, configure a new authentication connector for GitHub by creating a connector file `github.yaml` and executing `tctl create github.yaml`.
3. If you wish, you can also set GitHub to be the default authentication preference for a cluster.

That's basically it; after these steps, access to your infrastructure is only possible via GitHub SSO.

Managing Client Devices

Trusted devices provide an important layer of security in a Zero Trust environment by binding every device identity to a user. Access is granted only when both identities are present and verifiable at the same time. To become a trusted device, a laptop must have a secure enclave hardware capability. Device trust consists of two key concepts:

Inventory management

> This is the registration of devices with the Teleport cluster. This happens when the IT department of your company acquires new devices before they're issued to employees.

Device enrollment

> This happens when a device goes into use and is assigned to a user. The device enrollment process creates the secure enclave private key on the device and registers the corresponding public key with the Teleport cluster. Device enrollment establishes a bond between a user and a device.

The tie between the device inventory and enrollment is a device enrollment token. A device enrollment token needs to be created by a device admin and sent to the person performing the enrollment ceremony.

For example:

```
# Add a device to the cluster inventory:
$ tctl devices add -asset-tag="XYZ"
# To enroll a device, token must be generated by cluster admin:
$ tctl devices enroll -asset-tag="XYZ"
# To finish enrollment, a user executes this on the device:
$ tsh device enroll -token="secret-token"
```

Managing Permissions

The Teleport cluster is the single source of truth for infrastructure access policy within an organization. This involves two primary mechanisms: the role-based access control (RBAC) engine and the access workflows engine.

The RBAC engine works as follows:

1. Create user roles, either manually or using code. These roles apply to all infrastructure resource types.

2. Create a mapping between Teleport roles and the roles defined within an IdM. In our example, this means a mapping between Teleport roles and GitHub SSO.

3. Define policy by configuring each role for different infrastructure types. For example, a role can enable or disable SSH, restrict session length, map a role to local Linux or Windows accounts, map a role to Kubernetes groups, restrict access only to AWS resources with specific labels, and so on.

An access workflow can be defined to temporarily elevate user privileges based on arbitrary criteria such as attributes. Let's consider the following scenario using a Slack Teleport plug-in.

Imagine a user named Joe. Normally, Joe has no permissions to access a mission critical database. Access is controlled by a privileged role called db_admin. Most of the time, no users have this role.

If someone creates a support ticket asking a database administrator to look into an issue with the database, Joe gains access as follows:

1. Joe creates an access request in Teleport, specifying a reason (the ticket).

2. Teleport forwards the request to a Slack channel where another user with approval privileges can grant access by temporarily assigning the db_admin role to Joe.

3. Joe can now access the database and look at the issue.

4. When Joe disconnects, the db_admin role and its associated privileges are revoked.

By creating your own plug-ins, you can implement similar logic using a completely automated workflow. For example, users can be automatically granted additional privileges based on a support schedule or any other criteria.

Managing Audit

A Teleport cluster collects and stores all security-related information from all supported resource types in a consolidated audit log. The audit log contains two types of data: structured security events and interactive session recordings.

Security events include cluster logins, Linux or Windows machine logins, remote command executions, file transfers, database queries, or events from a Kubernetes audit log. These events can be stored in various configurable storage backends, such as DynamoDB, GCP Filestore, or a local filesystem.

The interactive sessions can be recorded for SSH, Windows sessions, and for interactive kubectl sessions to Kubernetes clusters. The command-line recordings are stored in the native ASCII format and can be compressed, while graphical Windows sessions require significantly more disk space. The session recordings can be stored on a local filesystem, in an AWS S3 bucket, or a similar cloud block storage service. You can use a forwarding agent like Fluentd or Logstash to export the audit log in to a SIEM solution such as Panther.

Zero Trust Configuration

Typical computing infrastructure listens on the network. In a cloud environment there are usually thousands of network sockets in a listening state, implementing protocols such as MySQL, SSH, RDP, PostgreSQL, and HTTPS. Implementing Zero Trust principles for all resources means that authentication, encryption, authorization, and audit must be enabled for all connections at all times. This means routing all connections through the proxy.

Teleport provides two ways to manage these connections: agent mode and agentless mode, each with its trade-offs. Using SSH as an example, here's how these modes are different:

Agent mode
> Each Linux box runs the Teleport Server Access service. The Teleport Server Access service agent does not listen on a network at all. Instead, it always maintains an outgoing encrypted tunnel to the Teleport proxy. Client connections are established through the tunnel.

Agentless mode
> A client connection goes through the Teleport proxy into a Linux machine that does not have a Teleport service on it. Instead, the connection is accepted by the sshd OpenSSH daemon that comes standard with nearly all Linux distributions.

Each of these modes has its own pros and cons. The agentless mode makes it easier to deploy and upgrade Teleport, because there is no need to deploy thousands of agents onto each machine. But this raises the administrative cost of maintaining the sshd configuration, making sure it can only trust clients with Teleport certificates.

On the other hand, the agent mode delivers true Zero Trust without any maintenance overhead. Nodes do not listen on the network at all, which means this mode can be used on public networks. Moreover, because all connectivity is established through a proxy, this allows connections to devices located on third-party networks behind NAT. This mode also allows full Zero Trust access to legacy workloads supporting only insecure protocols, for example to web applications without any authentication or encryptions that simply listen on localhost:80.

Living the Principles of Identity-Native Access

Integrating an identity-aware proxy with IdM provides a holistic view of the entire infrastructure by connecting all users, all infrastructure, and all client devices. The users are connected via SSO integration, while the resources and client devices are connected via enrollment. This is true identity-native access management because it requires a unique identity for all objects and subjects. With this approach, static credentials disappear. All client devices rely on their secure enclaves to authenticate, all servers use HSMs or single-use join tokens to join a cluster, and all users provide biometric proof. Identity transfer happens via ephemeral self-expiring certificates, and there is no private key material accessible to rogue humans or vulnerable applications. With no secrets to steal, perimeter-focused defense is no longer relevant.

Policy is defined for the whole infrastructure, treating the environment as if it were a single machine. Managed centrally by the reference monitor, policy becomes a kind of user interface to this imagined machine. This provides consistent access between all types of subjects and objects and prevents access silos from forming.

Consolidating audit in one place becomes automatic because all access events within a cluster are aggregated by the IAP and exported into a location well-suited for a SIEM integration such as AWS S3.

Defining access as code is perhaps the most challenging capability to achieve, because it involves automating numerous access-related tasks: onboarding and offboarding users, enrolling and removing devices and servers, elevating privileges based on external attributes, acquiring certificates programmatically for service accounts and microservices, and providing compatibility with all common DevOps practices. An effective access architecture supports automation that integrates with common DevOps tooling such as Ansible or Terraform or provides an API for invoking authentication capabilities directly.

Identity-native infrastructure access must be an integral part of any cloud native technology stack at scale. Cost effective scaling and ease of use are the keys to effective infrastructure security because these factors are most important in reducing incentives to engage in corner-cutting behaviors that lead to the one and only security risk: human error.

## CHAPTER 8

A Call to Action

In the previous chapters, we've talked a lot about what we don't want to allow: human error, vulnerabilities, attacks, and threats. But the point of the book is about access—letting people in, not shutting them out. We want people to be able to work together easily.

In fact, easy access is the whole point. While security and convenience are traditionally at odds with each other, inconvenience itself leads to cutting corners, then human error, and therefore to vulnerability. Convenience and security should be best friends, not rivals. The secure path must be a happy path.

The answer, my friends, is identity-native access.

Security and Convenience at Scale

When identity-native access is working properly, it's almost invisible to the user. Already, when you shop online, your browser trusts the marketplace with a certificate invisibly, without bothering you. Most people don't understand certificates because they don't have to; they never see them. They just work.

Meanwhile, in many large organizations, organically farmed access silos are resulting in the opposite: the most inconvenient security mechanisms possible. The forest of secrets, jump hosts, permissions, protocols, and schemas becomes a labyrinth of vulnerabilities for malicious actors to exploit. Meanwhile, the inconvenience of dealing with myriad invasive security rituals interferes with productivity and tempts people into careless behavior, making the problem even worse.

Bringing true identity to access control, reducing complexity, and eliminating both secrets and reliance on network boundaries, make security more manageable by making it easier. Unifying access control for humans, machines, and applications reduces the overhead required to maintain trust across all the different systems at scale. At the same time, this approach brings consistent visibility across the whole system. True identity-native access control gets security out of the way of the users so they don't take harmful shortcuts that undermine security policy.

Identity-native access doesn't require secrets to prove identity. As a result, because there are no secrets to protect, there's nothing left to exploit. Human error is rendered powerless. Because every access or action rests on the proven identities of the parties involved, you don't need to trust anyone by default. That means no enclave where everyone is trusted, which means no perimeter to defend. Trust is atomic and rests on proven identity. That is why an identity-native, Zero Trust access architecture scales so well: it only needs to scale linearly to meet the demands of each interaction, rather than patching up a geometrically scaled quilt of defenses against anticipated perimeter attacks on variegated platforms.

Imagine scaling these ideas up to encompass the entire internet itself.

The Future of Trust

In recent years, the internet has developed trust issues. We don't control our own data, which is scooped up and sold by social media and marketing companies—in fact, by every website we visit. The information presented on those websites is often unsourced at best, propaganda at worst. Even content that was considered the very standard of truth, such as photographs and video clips, can be faked convincingly. The internet is inherently untrustworthy: we can't rely on the truthfulness of information on the internet, or on the internet enforcing policy. Trust is eroding, and the tech companies are becoming pariahs.

While most information on the internet is still created by humans, it's now very easy and inexpensive to create new information using AI. You could build an entire copy of the internet, but with your own version of history, injecting or removing whatever you like. It would not be difficult, using AI, to create an alternate internet with no mention of the Holocaust. You could create ten, a hundred, a thousand internets of information according to your needs.

How can anyone know what's true?

To rebuild trust on the internet, trust has to be built into the very fabric of information. Every piece of data needs to be attached to an owner, so you know how you can trust it. That means every user needs to be identified in a way that works the same across the entire internet.

A centralized, federated identification for every user not only provides provenance for every piece of data but makes it possible to enforce policy as well. Imagine if you could set policy for every piece of data you create or own—or, in fact, for every bit of information about you. Imagine giving companies access to information with an expiration date, retaining control instead of letting corporations simply farm your information.

Remember Multics, which we talked about in Chapter 5? In Multics, the clever mechanism of segments makes it possible for data to enforce its own policy. Every piece of data is attached to an owner and policy that can't be circumvented.

This is the first step to gaining a holistic view of everything. Scaling this idea up, it can be possible to create a single source of policy for the entire internet. Users could set limits for the data that's collected about them and how it's used. This would help build public trust in companies. And because every piece of data has a defined owner—a provenance—it would be possible to verify the veracity of every piece of information, or at least assess the intention for which it was created.

Infrastructure as One Big Machine

Once you have a holistic view across your infrastructure (or the internet), the entire environment can behave as a single machine. A consistent, holistic view over the system, with a single source of policy that's enforced the same for all subjects and objects, brings a unity of vision and control. Identity-native access becomes a de facto user interface to the machine. This is the state we want to attain.

Once you have a unified interface that treats all your infrastructure as a single machine, you can deploy AI to give the machine instructions in natural language. Instead of the old way, where DevOps engineers log in to an army of servers, clusters, and databases to issue instructions on the command line, you can just ask your infrastructure questions or give commands in your native language. What are the bottlenecks to run this SQL query? When was the last time we did a backup of all production data? Is anyone on my team accessing any resources at the moment?

Once you use the principles of identity-native access architecture to gain a single view across your entire infrastructure, you open up the possibility of speaking to your whole world naturally. Otherwise, you're left running a patchwork of antiquated systems, and won't be able to take advantage of the AI advances to come.

The Future of Security Threats

AI won't just revolutionize the way you manage your infrastructure. Threat actors are already using AI to refine attacks and develop new ones.

Let's take phishing as an example. Every phishing attack relies on a familiar medium, such as an email from your boss's address, and a context intended to convince you the medium is legitimate. Let's say your company has a sales meeting every Friday where the best salesperson gets a weekly award. An email seemingly from your boss might ask you to click a link to claim your award. This context lowers your guard, making it more likely that you'll ignore errors in the medium—as Marshall McLuhan would say, the message itself—and click the link.

AI makes it much easier for attackers to gather the context they can use in phishing attacks. With AI, they can look at every company's social media presence, monitor email traffic, and look at other conversations to understand what's happening—and what else can be exploited.

The threat industry has long been an arms race between security professionals and attackers. New technology becomes available, often first on the attack side, and security learns to deal with it. One side is always ahead of the other: sometimes security is winning, but then a new attack becomes available. At these times, everyone is vulnerable and uncomfortable.

Because humans are always the weakest link, attackers are already starting to use generative AI to craft more sophisticated phishing attacks. AI can write very convincing emails in massive numbers—or even call your phone and talk to you using a deepfake of your boss's voice. With the right context and the right knowledge about you, an attack can be very convincing and effective.

The impulse is to use AI as a security tool, to fight fire with fire. The security industry can respond with AI-driven systems that look at audit logs to detect the presence of things that look like threats. The fact is, however, that this is just a continuation of the arms race. The attackers' AI will win some of the time.

Instead, this book has proposed stepping out of the arms race altogether. By not relying on secrets, identity-native infrastructure access architecture leaves little to gain by phishing. If access doesn't rely on secrets, then phishing can't provide access.

Closing Words

This book is an urgent call to action. The current state of information and infrastructure access leaves the door open to exploitation: infrastructure attacks, phishing, disinformation, and cyberterrorism. Advances in AI and other technology will continue, and the target remains the same: human error. When the defenses against these attacks rely on humans, human error is a constant vulnerability. Identity-native access takes humans, and human error, completely out of the access process. By automating access completely, you become immune to human error. That is what identity-native access control is all about.

Index

About the Authors

Ev Kontsevoy is cofounder and CEO of Teleport. An engineer by training, Kontsevoy launched Teleport in 2015 to provide other engineers solutions that allow them to quickly access and run any computing resource anywhere on the planet without having to worry about security and compliance issues. A serial entrepreneur, Ev was CEO and cofounder of Mailgun, which he successfully sold to Rackspace. Prior to Mailgun, Ev has had a variety of engineering roles. He holds a BS degree in Mathematics from Siberian Federal University, and has a passion for trains and vintage-film cameras.

Sakshyam Shah is a cybersecurity architect by profession and currently an engineer at Teleport. Besides cybersecurity, he loves to read and write about indie hackers, bootstrapped businesses, and early-stage venture funding.

Peter Conrad is an author, artist, and technical content strategist with experience ranging from consumer electronics and telecommunications to IoT and enterprise software.

Colophon

The animal on the cover of *Identity-Native Infrastructure Access Management* is a common warthog (*Phacochoerus africanus*). A member of the pig family (*Suidae*), these warthogs are often found roaming the savanna grasslands, open bushlands, and woodlands in sub-Saharan Africa.

Common warthogs live in small groups known as sounders. Although they can dig their own burrows, warthogs prefer to occupy abandoned burrows of aardvarks and other animals. They spend much of their day foraging, feeding on grasses and green shoots; in drier weather, they dig for roots and seeds using their large snouts. Their most identifiable feature is their pair of tusks, which they use to fight against predators like lions, leopards, cheetahs, and hyenas. Although common warthogs are not an endangered species, they are susceptible to drought and overhunting, which may lead to a decline in their population.

Many of the animals on O'Reilly covers are endangered; all of them are important to the world.

The cover illustration is by Karen Montgomery, based on an antique line engraving from *Cassell's Natural History*. The cover fonts are Gilroy Semibold and Guardian Sans. The text font is Adobe Minion Pro; the heading font is Adobe Myriad Condensed; and the code font is Dalton Maag's Ubuntu Mono.

O'REILLY®

Learn from experts.
Become one yourself.

Books | Live online courses
Instant answers | Virtual events
Videos | Interactive learning

Get started at oreilly.com.

Printed in the USA
CPSIA information can be obtained
at www.ICGtesting.com
JSHW062151050224
56676JS00012B/191

9 781098 131890